YOUNG IMPACT ONE

Young Impact One

R. H. POOLE
Senior Lecturer in English,
Wolverhampton Teachers' College

AND

P. J. SHEPHERD
Senior Lecturer in English,
Eastbourne College of Education

HEINEMANN EDUCATIONAL
BOOKS LTD · LONDON

Heinemann Educational Books Ltd
LONDON EDINBURGH MELBOURNE TORONTO
JOHANNESBURG SINGAPORE NEW DELHI
AUCKLAND HONG KONG
IBADAN NAIROBI
KUALA LUMPUR

ISBN 0 435 10704 6

Published by
Heinemann Educational Books Ltd
48 Charles Street, London W1X 8AH
Filmset by Keyspools Ltd, Golborne, Lancashire
Printed in Great Britain by
C. Tinling & Co. Ltd, Prescot and London

CONTENTS

LIST OF ILLUSTRATIONS

Cover photograph by John Krish

THEMES AND TOPICS

RHYTHM

Godolphin Horne

Godolphin Horne was Nobly Born;
He held the Human Race in Scorn,
And lived with all his Sisters where
His Father lived, in Berkeley Square.
And oh! the Lad was Deathly Proud!

He never shook your Hand or Bowed,
But merely smirked and nodded thus:
How perfectly ridiculous!
Alas! That such Affected Tricks
Should flourish in a Child of Six!
(For such was Young Godolphin's age).
Just then, the Court required a Page,
Whereat the Lord High Chamberlain
(The Kindest and the Best of Men),
He went good-naturedly and took
A Perfectly Enormous Book
Called *People Qualified to Be*
Attendant on His Majesty,
And murmured, as he scanned the list
(To see that no one should be missed),
'There's William Coutts has got the Flu,
And Billy Higgs would never do,
And Guy de Vere is far too young,
And . . . wasn't D'Alton's Father hung?
And as for Alexander Byng!— . . .
I think I know the kind of thing,
A Churchman, cleanly, nobly born,
Come let us say Godolphin Horne?'
But hardly had he said the word
When Murmurs of Dissent were heard.
The King of Iceland's Eldest Son
Said, 'Thank you! I am taking none!'
The Aged Duchess of Athlone

Remarked, in her sub-acid tone,
'I doubt if He is what we need!'
With which the Bishops all agreed;
And even Lady Mary Flood
(*So* Kind, and oh! so *really* Good)
Said, 'No! He wouldn't do at all,
He'd make us feel a lot too small.'
The Chamberlain said, '. . . Well, well, well!
No doubt you're right . . . One cannot tell!'
He took his Gold and Diamond Pen
And scratched Godolphin out again.
So now Godolphin is the Boy
Who blacks the Boots at the Savoy.

HILAIRE BELLOC

Edward Franks

Here is the tale of Edward Franks,
Who often played some silly pranks,
Like putting cushions on the door,
And smearing soap upon the floor,
Till his relations all agreed,
A smacking was young Edward's need.
Alas, his doting mother said,
'Clever I think it is of Ted,
To think up all these funny jokes,
He does it to amuse you folks,
He does not do it to annoy.
He really is a charming boy.'
One day his Uncle Robert, who
Had fought the Boer, and Zulu, too,
Invited Ted to come and stay,
Thinking, 'At last this is the day,
To knock out of his silly head,
The prankish thoughts of foolish Ted!'
He came, and soon he went to rest,
A thing which Edward did detest,
When suddenly he thought, 'My sheet
Will cover me from head to feet.
So like a ghost I then look will

'Twill make my Uncle Bob grow chill.'
The sheet he hastily put on,
No light in Uncle's room there shone,
He crept up to his Uncle's bed,
And softly touched his Uncle's head,
And then retreated to the door;
But Uncle naughty Edward saw,
And, taking him for robber bad,
Ejaculated a 'By Gad!'
And pulled a pistol from his drawer
And shot. Alas! it was before
His horrible mistake he found,
Poor Edward lay upon the ground.
The bullet had gone through his head,
The wretched youngster lay there, dead.

A boy aged 12

A Ruthless Rhyme

Auntie, did you feel no pain
Falling from that apple-tree?
Will you do it, please, again?
'Cos my friend here didn't see.

HARRY GRAHAM

Adventures of Isabel

Isabel met an enormous bear,
Isabel, Isabel, didn't care;
The bear was hungry, the bear was ravenous,
The bear's big mouth was cruel and cavernous.
The bear said, Isabel, glad to meet you,
How do, Isabel, now I'll eat you!
Isabel, Isabel, didn't worry,
Isabel didn't scream or scurry.
She washed her hands and she straightened her hair up,
Then Isabel quietly ate the bear up.

Once in a night as black as pitch
Isabel met a wicked old witch.

The witch's face was cross and wrinkled,
The witch's gums with teeth were sprinkled.
Ho, ho, Isabel! the old witch crowed,
I'll turn you into an ugly toad!
Isabel, Isabel, didn't worry,
Isabel didn't scream or scurry,
She showed no rage and she showed no rancour,
But she turned the witch into milk and drank her.

Isabel met a hideous giant,
Isabel continued self-reliant.
The giant was hairy, the giant was horrid,
He had one eye in the middle of his forehead.
Good morning Isabel, the giant said,
I'll grind your bones to make my bread.
Isabel, Isabel, didn't worry,
Isabel didn't scream or scurry.
She nibbled the zwieback[1] that she always fed off,
And when it was gone, she cut the giant's head off.

Isabel met a troublesome doctor,
He punched and he poked till he really shocked her.
The doctor's talk was of coughs and chills
And the doctor's satchel bulged with pills.
The doctor said unto Isabel,
Swallow this, it will make you well.
Isabel, Isabel, didn't worry,
Isabel didn't scream or scurry.
She took those pills from the pill concocter,
And Isabel calmly cured the doctor.

OGDEN NASH

Sir Roger is Dead

Sir Roger is dead and gone to his grave,
Mm, ha, gone to his grave.
They planted an apple tree over his head,
Mm, ha, over his head.
The apples are ripe and ready to drop,
Mm, ha, ready to drop.

[1] A kind of biscuit, rusk or sweet cake toasted in slices.

There came an old woman a-picking them up,
Mm, ha, picking them up.
Sir Roger got up and gave her a knock,
Mm, ha, gave her a knock.
Which made the old woman go hippity hop,
Mm, ha, hippity hop.
Ena, mena, mo, tisn't you shall go.
It's you, it's you, it's you.
Now I dare you, I dare you.
Take an apple, steal a bullseye.
Cowardly, cowardly custard,
Your eye stings of mustard.
Cry baby creep, Phoebe lies asleep.
Steal an apple, she won't hurt you.
Take a bullseye, she can't touch you.
I dare you, I dare you.

MARGARET STANLEY-WRENCH
from *An Old Woman Remembering*

Child's Bouncing Song

Molly Vickers
wets her knickers,
Georgie's father's big and black,
cream on Sunday
milk on Monday,
I'm the cock of all the back.

Tell me who's a
bigger boozer
Mister Baker beats them all,
from his lorry
watch him hurry,
touch the ground and touch the wall.

Who're the gentry
down our entry –
Mrs Smith's got two TVs.
What if her coat
is a fur coat,
all her kids are full of fleas.

Joan loves Harry,
Jack will marry
Edna when they both grow up,
I'll announce it,
bounce bounce bounce it,
our dog Whisker's had a pup.

High and low and
to and fro and
down the street and up the hill,
Mrs Cuthbert's
husband snuffed it,
she got nothing from his will.

Mister, mister,
Shirley's sister
won a prize on Blackpool prom,
mam'll smother
our kid brother
when the school inspectors come.

Skip and hopping
I'm off shopping
Tuesday night it's pie for tea,
please to take this
ball and make this
song of bouncing song for me.

TONY CONNOR

Narnian Suite

With plucking pizzicato and the prattle of the kettledrum
We're trotting into battle mid a clatter of accoutrement;
Our beards are big as periwigs and trickle with opopanax,[1]
And trinketry and treasure twinkle out on every part of us –
        (Scrape! Tap! The fiddle and the kettledrum).

The chuckle-headed humans think we're only petty
        poppetry
And all our battle-tackle nothing more than pretty bric-a-
        brac;
[1] Gum resin.

But a little shrub has prickles, and they'll soon be in a
   pickle if
A scud of dwarfish archery has crippled all their cavalry –
      (Whizz! Twang! The quarrel and the javelin).

And when the tussle thickens we can writhe and wriggle
   under it;
Then dagger-point'll tickle 'em, and grab and grip'll
   grapple 'em,
And trap and trick'll trouble 'em and tackle 'em and topple
   'em
Till they're huddled, all be-diddled, in the middle of our
   caperings –
      (Dodge! Jump! The wriggle and the summersault).

When we've scattered 'em and peppered 'em with pebbles
   from our catapults
We'll turn again in triumph and by crannies and by
   crevices
Go back to where the capitol and cradle of our people is,
Our forges and our furnaces, the caverns of the earth –
      (Gold! Fire! The anvil and the smithying).

March for Drum, Trumpet, and Twenty-one Giants

                    With stumping stride in pomp and pride
                    We come to thump and floor ye;
                    We'll bump your lumpish heads today
                    And tramp your ramparts into clay,
                    And as we stamp and romp and play
                    Our trump'll blow before us –
   (crescendo)   Oh tramp it, tramp it, tramp it, trumpet,
                       trumpet blow before us!

                    We'll grind and break and bind and take
                    And plunder ye and pound ye!
                    With trundled rocks and bludgeon blow,
                    You dunderheads, we'll dint ye so
                    You'll blunder and run blind, as though
                    By thunder stunned, around us –
                    By thunder, thunder, thunder, thunder,
                       thunder stunned around us!

Ho! tremble town and tumble down
And crumble shield and sabre!
Your kings will mumble and look pale,
Your horses stumble or turn tail,
Your skimble-scamble counsels fail,
So rumble drum belaboured –
(diminuendo)   Oh rumble, rumble, rumble, rumble,
rumble drum belaboured!

C. S. LEWIS

The Great Panjandrum

So she went into the garden
to cut a cabbage-leaf
to make an apple-pie;
and at the same time

a great she-bear, coming down the street,
pops its head into the shop.
What! no soap?
So he died,
and she very imprudently married the Barber:
and there were present
the Picninnies,
and the Joblillies,
And the Garyulies,
and the great Panjandrum himself,
with the little round button at top;
and they all fell to playing the game of catch-as-catch-can,
till the gunpowder ran out at the heels of their boots.

SAMUEL FOOTE

PEOPLE

My Brother Bert

Pets are the Hobby of my brother Bert,
He used to go to school with a Mouse in his shirt.

His Hobby it grew, as some hobbies will,
And grew and GREW and GREW until –

Oh don't breathe a word, pretend you haven't heard.
A simply appalling thing has occurred –

The very thought makes me iller and iller:
Bert's brought home a gigantic Gorilla!

If you think that's really not such a scare,
What if it quarrels with his Grizzly Bear?

You still think you could keep your head?
What if the Lion from under the bed

And the four Ostriches that deposit
Their football eggs in his bedroom closet

And the Aardvark out of his bottom drawer
All danced out and joined in the Roar?

What if the Pangolins were to caper
Out of their nests behind the wallpaper?

With the fifty sort of Bats
That hang on his hatstand like old hats,

And out of a shoebox the excitable Platypus
Along with the Ocelot or Jungle-Cattypus?

The Wombat, the Dingo, the Gecko, the Grampus –
How would they shake the house with their Rumpus?

Not to forget the Bandicoot
Who would certainly peer from his battered old boot.

Why it could be a dreadful day,
And what Oh what would the neighbours say!

TED HUGHES

My Grandpa

The truth of the matter, the truth of the matter—
As one who supplies us with hats is a Hatter,
As one who is known for his growls is a Growler—
My grandpa traps owls, yes, my grandpa's an Owler.

Though owls, alas, are quite out of fashion,
Grandpa keeps busy about his profession
And hoards every owl that falls to his traps:
'Someday,' he says, 'they'll be needed, perhaps.'

'Owls are such sages,' he says, 'I surmise
Listening to owls could make the world wise.'
Nightlong his house is shaken with hoots,
And he wakes to owls in his socks and his boots.

Owls, owls, nothing but owls,
The most fantastical of fowls;

White owls from the Arctic, black owls from the Tropic.
Some are far-sighted, others myopic.

There are owls on his picture frame, owls on his chairs,
Owls in dozens ranked on his stairs.
Eyes, eyes, rows of their eyes.
Some are big as collie dogs, some are thumb-size.

Deep into Africa, high into Tibet
He travels with his rubber mouse and wiry owl-net;
The rarest of owls, and the very most suspicious
Will pounce on a mouse and be tangled in the meshes.

'Whatever you could wish to know, an owl will surely
                                        know it,'
My grandpa says proudly, 'And how does he show it?
Sleeping and thinking and sleeping and thinking—
Letting a horrible hoot out and winking!'

                                        TED HUGHES

My Sister Jane

And I say nothing – no, not a word
About our Jane. Haven't you heard?
She's a bird, a bird, a bird, a bird.
Oh it never would do to let folks know
My sister's nothing but a great big crow.

Each day (we daren't send her to school)
She pulls on stockings of thick blue wool
To make her pin crow legs look right,
Then fits a wig of curls on tight,
And dark spectacles – a huge pair
To cover her very crowy stare.
Oh it never would do to let folks know
My sister's nothing but a great big crow.

When visitors come she sits upright
(With her wings and her tail tucked out of sight).
They think her queer but extremely polite.
Then when the visitors have gone

She whips out her wings and with her wig on
Whirls through the house at the height of your head –
Duck, duck, or she'll knock you dead.
Oh it never would do to let folks know
My sister's nothing but a great big crow.

At meals whatever she sees she'll stab it –
Because she's a crow and that's a crow habit.
My mother says, 'Jane! Your manners! Please!'
Then she'll sit quietly on the cheese,
Or play the piano nicely by dancing on the keys –
Oh it never would do to let folks know
My sister's nothing but a great big crow.

TED HUGHES

Bull Chadwick

It was among the boys that trouble was stirring and the cause
of it all was a furnaceman in the forge – a man called Chadwick,
who, because of his short thick neck set in massive shoulders,
and the coarse red curls of wiry hair growing low on his forehead, was nicknamed Bull.

Bull was a strange sort of fellow. He was the strongest
man in the forge, and he was proud of his strength. Not that
he went around showing his muscles and boasting about it,
but whenever there was any lifting to be done he always took
the heavy end; and one day when one of the gang was hurt
by the shaft of a breaking cutter, Bull carried him all the
way to the hospital in his arms like a child. Sometimes in
working a job a badly timed 'shove' from the press would
make a small flaw, called a 'lap' in the forging. This would
have to be cut out immediately, and while the forgeman
held the long-handled chisel, it was always Bull who swung
the hammer. There he would stand, close up to the glowing
steel, his feet widespread and the fourteen-pound hammer
whirling in a perfect circle. His great red hairy hands gripped
the very end of the haft and never shifted an inch; and his
eyes would be shining and there would be a look of real
happiness in his face. It was one of the special sights of Valley
Forge to see Bull Chadwick swing a sledge.

He used his strength in other ways too, and if any of the

gang had furniture to shift or a particularly hard and stony patch in his garden to dig, the Bull was always ready and eager to help.

All the men liked him, but for some reason he just could not stand the boys. He was always plaguing them with nasty little tricks, and some that were even dangerous. Booby traps with water or a filthy mixture of oil and soot were his favourites; but there were others equally unpleasant, and when all else failed, he was not above using his great strength to put some unoffending errand boy into a state of misery and discomfort.

So far he had got away with it. True, now and then one of his victims would retaliate by hacking his shins, but he was such a powerful brute that the idea of hitting back at him didn't occur to the lads. Generally they kept as far away from him as possible, and were ready to jump whenever he was in sight. For the rest, they had to put up with Bull Chadwick as something inevitable – like the heat and the noise.

RICHARD ARMSTRONG, *Sabotage at the Forge*

The Rose-Beetle Man

Perhaps one of the most weird and fascinating characters I met during my travels was the Rose-Beetle Man. He had a fairytale air about him that was impossible to resist, and I used to look forward eagerly to my infrequent meetings with him. I first saw him on a high, lonely road leading to one of the remote mountain villages. I could hear him long before I could see him, for he was playing a rippling tune on a shepherd's pipe, breaking off now and then to sing a few words in a curious, nasal voice. As he rounded the corner both Roger and I stopped and stared at him in amazement.

He had a sharp, fox-like face with large, slanting eyes of such a dark brown that they appeared black. They had a weird, vacant look about them, and a sort of bloom such as one finds on a plum, a pearly covering almost like a cataract. He was short and slight, with a thinness about his wrists and neck that argued a lack of food. His dress was fantastic, and on his head was a shapeless hat with a very wide, floppy brim. It had once been bottle-green, but was now speckled and smeared with dust, wine-stains, and cigarette burns. In the band were stuck a fluttering forest of feathers: cock-feathers, hoopoe-feathers, owl-feathers, the wing of a kingfisher, the claw of a hawk, and a large dirty white feather that may have come from a swan. His shirt was worn and frayed, grey with sweat, and round the neck dangled an enormous cravat of the most startling blue satin. His coat was dark and shapeless, with patches of different hues here and there; on the sleeve a bit of white cloth with a design of rosebuds; on the shoulder a triangular patch of wine-red and white spots. The pockets of this garment bulged, the contents almost spilling out: combs, balloons, little highly coloured pictures of the saints, olive-wood carvings of snakes, camels, dogs and horses, cheap mirrors, a riot of handkerchiefs, and long twisted rolls of bread decorated with seeds. His trousers, patched like his coat, drooped over a pair of scarlet *charouhias*, leather shoes with upturned toes decorated with a large black-and-white pompon. This extraordinary character carried on his back bamboo cages full of pigeons and young chickens, several mysterious sacks, and a large bunch of fresh green leeks. With one hand he held his pipe to his mouth, and in the other a number of lengths of cotton, to each of which was tied an almond-size rose-beetle, glittering golden green in the sun, all of them flying round his hat with desperate, deep buzzings, trying to escape from the thread tied firmly round their waists. Occasionally, tired of circling round and round without success, one of the beetles would settle for a moment on his hat before launching itself off once more on its endless merry-go-round.

GERALD DURRELL, *My Family and Other Animals*

Dr Goat

So Don Alonso made up his mind to send his son to boarding-school, both to prevent him from being spoiled at home and to save himself worry. He found out that there was a certain Dr Goat in Segovia who tutored gentlemen's sons. So he sent his son there and me as well to be his companion and servant.

The first Sunday after Lent we fell into the power of Hunger incarnate. I could never exaggerate the sufferings he caused us. He was in holy orders, as skinny as a pea-shooter, generous only in height, with a small head and ginger hair. I need say no more, if you remember that Judas had red hair. His eyes were sunk so deep in his head that they were like lamps at the end of a cave; so sunken and dark that they looked like a draper's window. His nose was partly Roman and partly French, because it was poxy with cold sores . . . His whiskers were pale, scared stiff of his starving mouth which was threatening to gnaw them. I don't know how many of his teeth he had missing: I suppose he had dismissed them as there was never any work for them to do. His neck was as long as an ostrich's and his Adam's apple looked as if it had been forced to go and look for food. His arms were withered and his hands were like dried-up vine shoots. His legs looked like the prongs of a fork or a pair of skinny dividers. He walked very slowly. If he rushed for any reason his bones rattled like the clappers that hospital charity collectors rattle in the streets; his voice was hollow and he had a long beard because he wouldn't spend money on shaving and, in any case, he said the barber's hands on his face made him feel sick and he'd rather die than feel them. One of the other boys used to cut his hair for him. When the weather was hot he wore a hat chewed all over by the cat and decorated with grease spots. It was made of something that had once been cloth and was well-lined with scurf. Some said his cassock was miraculous because nobody could tell its colour. As it had no nap left some said it was made of frog's skin; others said it was an optical illusion as it looked black from close up but bluish from a distance. He had no belt, collar or cuffs. With his long hair and short skimpy cassock he looked like the Angel of Death in person. Goliath's coffin could have fitted into each of his shoes. And his room! There weren't even any spiders there. He put a spell on the mice in case they nibbled the few crumbs he hoarded. He slept on the floor on one side so as not to wear out the sheets. In short he was the High Priest of Poverty and Avarice incarnate.

So I fell into his hands together with Don Diego. On the day we arrived he showed us our room and made us a little speech; little, to save time. He told us what we were to do and this took us until lunch time. The refectory was terribly small but it contained about five young gentlemen. First, I looked round to see if there were any cats and, as there were not, I asked an old servant why not.

He bore the mark of the place on his emaciated body. He softened and said:

'What do you mean, cats? Who told you cats like fasting and

penance? It's not hard to see you're new; you won't stay fat for long!' When I heard that I began to get nervous and I got even more scared when I saw that the others looked as skinny as rakes with faces which looked as if they had been plastered with white lead. Dr Goat sat down and said grace. Then our masters ate an infinite meal, by which I mean it had no beginning and no end. They brought little wooden bowls of a soup so clear that if Narcissus had drunk it he would have fallen in quicker than into the pool. With a pain in my chest I saw the lean fingers paddling after one lone, orphaned chick pea at the bottom of the bowl. After each sip, Dr Goat said:

'Yes, they can say what they like, there's nothing like stew. All the rest is luxury and greed.' And as he said it he slopped his soup greedily, saying:

'It's all goodness and food!'

'I hope it chokes you,' I said under my breath when I saw a listless servant with a plate of meat in his hands. He was so thin that it looked as if the meat had come off his own bones. Up came a brave pioneering turnip and Dr Goat said:

'Turnips today? Partridges have nothing on them. Eat up now, I love seeing how you enjoy your food!'

He shared out such a tiny piece of mutton that, between what got caught under the nails and between the teeth, there was nothing left and our masters' guts were not admitted to the sacrament. Dr Goat looked at them and said:

'Eat up! You're young lads and I like to see a healthy appetite.'

Marvellous encouragement if hunger is gnawing at you already, isn't it?

After the meal a few crumbs were left on the table and some skin and bones on a plate. Our tutor said:

'Leave that for the servants. They must eat too and we shouldn't be greedy.'

'I hope God makes you choke on your food, you mean old bastard,' I muttered. 'Fancy insulting my belly like that!'

He said grace and then:

'Right, let the servants sit down and you go and take some exercise until two o'clock to make sure you digest what you've eaten properly.'

At that I could not help laughing and I roared. He became very annoyed and told me I should learn to be humble, as well as two or three other old maxims. We sat down and I saw that

this was a bad business and my guts were grumbling. Being craftier than the rest I grabbed the plate first and gobbled up two of the three crumbs as well as the single piece of skin. The others began to protest and, hearing the noise, in ran Goat saying:

'Eat like brothers! God has provided! Don't fight, there's enough for all.'

FRANCISCO DE QUEVEDO, translated MICHAEL ALPERT, *The Swindler*

JOBS

At the Butcher's

A visit to the butcher was very different. Here was all raw bloodiness and sawdust. The butcher's shop, which has now – like Turner's – disappeared, used to be near the corner farther down the High Street. The butcher's man had a large red nose in a thin red face covered with a lacy network of capillaries which made it look like rather coarse stewing steak. This im-

pression was enhanced by his carnivorous habits. Whenever
he cut up steak he would put a bit into his mouth as though it
were chocolate. Chewing and sucking, he sometimes managed
to swallow this and grab another and push it in, before dump-
ing the bulk on the scales. If it was too heavy, he put the sur-
plus in a little pile beside the scales, and we guessed what
would happen to that! Staring at him, open-mouthed, one
half of us saw him as human and felt sick; the other as a dog,
or a lion at meat . . .

GERALDINE SYMONS, *Children in the Close*

Bags of Meat

'Here's a fine bag of meat,'
Says the master-auctioneer,
As the timid, quivering steer,
Starting a couple of feet
At the prod of a drover's stick,
And trotting lightly and quick,
A ticket stuck on his rump,
Enters with a bewildered jump.

'Where he's lived lately, friends,
I'd live till lifetime ends:
They've a whole life everyday
Down there in the Vale, have they!
He'd be worth the money to kill
And give away Christmas for good-will.'

'Now here's a heifer – worth more
Than bid, were she bone-poor;
Yet she's round as a barrel of beer.'
'She's a plum,' said the second auctioneer.

'Now this young bull – for thirty pound?
Worth that to manure your ground!'
'Or to stand,' chimed the second one,
'And have his picter done!'

The beast was rapped on the horns and snout
To make him turn about.

'Well,' cried a buyer, 'another crown –
Since I've dragged here from Taunton Town!'

'That calf, she sucked three cows,
   Which is not matched for bouse[1]
   In the nurseries of high life
By the first-born of a nobleman's wife!'
The stick falls, meaning, 'A true tale's told,'
On the buttock of the creature sold,
   And the buyer leans over and snips
His mark on one of the animal's hips.

   Each beast, when driven in,
Looks round at the ring of bidders there
With a much-amazed reproachful stare,
   As at unnatural kin,
For bringing him to a sinister scene
So strange, unhomelike, hungry, mean;
His fate the while suspended between
   A butcher, to kill out of hand,
   And a farmer, to keep on the land;
One can fancy a tear runs down his face
When the butcher wins, and he's driven from the place.

                                   THOMAS HARDY

The Forge

All I know is a door into the dark.
Outside, old axles and iron hoops rusting;
Inside, the hammered anvil's short-pitched ring,
The unpredictable fantail of sparks
Or hiss when a new shoe toughens in water.
The anvil must be somewhere in the centre,
Horned as a unicorn, at one end square,
Set there immoveable: an altar
Where he expends himself in shape and music.
Sometimes, leather-aproned, hairs in his nose,
He leans out on the jamb, recalls a clatter
Of hoofs where traffic is flashing in rows;

[1]Drink.

Then grunts and goes in, with a slam and flick
To beat real iron out, to work the bellows.

SEAMUS HEANEY

The Carpenter

With a jack plane in his hands
My father the carpenter
Massaged the wafering wood,
Making it white and true.

He was skilful with his saws,
Handsaw, bowsaw, hacksaw,
And ripsaw with fishes' teeth
That chewed a plank in a second.

He was fond of silver bits,
The twist and countersink –
And the auger in its pit
Chucking shavings over its shoulder.

I remember my father's hands,
For they were supple and strong
With fingers that were lovers –
Sensuous strokers of wood:

He fondled the oak, the strong-man
Who holds above his head
A record-breaking lift
Of thick commingled boughs;

And he touched with his finger tips
Dark boards of elm and alder,
Spruce, and cherry for lathes
That turned all days to spring.

My father's hands were tender
Upon my tender head,
But they were massive on massive
Beam for building a house,

And delicate on the box wood
Leaning against the wall
As though placed there in a corner
For a moment and then forgotten,

And expert as they decoded
Archives unlocked by the axe –
The pretty medullary rays[1]
Once jammed with a traffic of food

To a watched and desired tree
That he marked and felled in the winter,
The tracks of tractors smashing
The ground where violets grew,

Then bound in chains and dragged
To the slaughtering circular saw:
A railway dulcimer
Rang the passing bell

Of my father's loved ones,
Though there was no grief in him
Caressing the slim wood, hearing
A robin's piccolo song.

                                   CLIFFORD DYMENT

Old Florist

That hump of a man bunching chrysanthemums
Or pinching-back asters, or planting azaleas,
Tamping and stamping dirt into pots, –
How he could flick and pick
Rotten leaves or yellowy petals,
Or scoop out a weed close to flourishing roots,
Or make the dust buzz with a light spray,
Or drown a bug in one spit of tobacco juice,
Or fan life into wilted sweet-peas with his hat,
Or stand all night watering roses, his feet blue in rubber
    boots.

                                   THEODORE ROETHKE

[1] Bands of cells which run (like rays) from the centre towards the circumference of
the tree trunk. They cut across the 'rings' by which one can tell the age of a tree.

TRADITIONAL

Jeanette Brunette

Jeanette Brunette
Had a wooden leg.
Her mother beat her,
And set her to beg.
She begged for meat
She begged for bread.
They gave her swine's feet
And a spoiled cabbage head.
She begged for gold.
They gave her a nail.
The nail made her bold.
She hid it in a pail.
When her mother was asleep
She drove it in her head.
She didn't cry a bit
When her mother lay dead.

KENNETH REXROTH from *Mother Goose*

The Wife of Usher's Well

There lived a wife at Usher's Well
    And a wealthy wife was she;
She had three stout and stalwart sons
    And sent them o'er the sea.

They hadna been a week from her,
    A week but barely ane,
Whan word came to the carline[1] wife
    That her three sons were gane.[2]

They hadna been a week from her,
    A week but barely three,
Whan word came to the carline wife
    That her sons she'd never see.

[1] old (woman).
[2] gone, dead.

25

I wish the wind may never cease,
   Nor fishes in the flood,
Till my three sons come hame to me
   In earthly flesh and blood.

It fell about the Martinmas
   Whan nights are lang and mirk,[1]
The carline wife's three sons came hame
   And their hats were o' the birk.[2]

It neither grew in syke[3] nor ditch
   Nor yet in ony sheugh,[4]
But at the gates o' Paradise
   That birk grew fair eneugh.

Blow up the fire, my maidens,
   Bring water from the well;
For a' my house shall feast this night
   Since my three sons are well.

And she has made to them a bed,
   She's made it large and wide,
And she's ta'en her mantle her about,
   Sat down at the bed-side.

Up then crew[5] the red, red cock
   And up and crew the gray;
The eldest to the youngest said,
   'Tis time we were away.

The cock he hadna craw'd but once
   And clapp'd his wings at a'
Whan the youngest to the eldest said,
   Brother, we must awa'.

The cock doth craw, the day doth daw,
   The channerin'[6] worm doth chide;
Gin we be mist out o' our place
   A sair pain we maun bide.

[1] dark.
[2] birch.
[3] small stream.
[4] trench.
[5] recalling the dead.
[6] fretting, grumbling (in the grave).

Fare ye weel, my mother dear;
  Fareweel to barn and byre;
And fare ye weel, the bonny lass
  That kindles my mother's fire.

ANON

Sir Patrick Spence

The king sits in Dumferling toune,
  Drinking the blude-reid wine:
O quhar[1] will I get [a] guid sailor,
  To sail this schip of mine?

Up and spak an eldern[2] knicht,
  Sat at the kings richt kne:
Sir Patrick Spence is the best sailor,
  That sails upon the se.

The king has written a braid[3] letter,
  And sign'd it wi' his hand;
And sent it to Sir Patrick Spence,
  Was walking on the sand.

The first line that Sir Patrick red,
  A loud lauch lauched he:
The next line that Sir Patrick red,
  The teir blinded his e'e.

O quha[4] is this has done this deid,
  This ill deid don to me;
To send me out this time o' the yeir,
  To sail upon the se?

Mak haste, mak haste, my mirry men all,
  Our guid schip sails the morne.
O say na sae, my master deir,
  For I feir a deadlie storme.

Late, late yestreen[5] I saw the new moone
  Wi' the auld moone in hir arme;
And I feir, I feir, my deir master,
  That we will com to harme.

[1] where.
[2] old.   [4] who.
[3] broad, long.   [5] last evening.

O our Scots nobles wer richt laith[1]
    To weet their cork-heil'd schoone;
Bot lang owre[2] a' the play wer play'd,
    Thair hats they swam aboone[3]

O lang, lang may thair ladies sit
    Wi' thair fans into their hand,
Or eir[4] they se Sir Patrick Spence
    Cum sailing to the land.

O lang, lang may the ladies stand
    Wi' their gold kems[5] in their hair,
Waiting for thair ain deir lords,
    For they'll se thame na mair.

Haf owre,[6] haf owre to Aberdour,[7]
    It's fiftie fadom deip:
And thair lies guid Sir Patrick Spence,
    Wi' the Scots lords at his feit.

AN

Ballad of the Frog Princess

A young prince rode the partridge wood,
    One hand on his bright thigh,
The other reined his sprinting mare
    As he passed by.
'Why do you range the woods,' I cried,
    'Where sullen thickets claw?
For unprotected is your heart,
    And your wounds raw.'

'Here I shall find my love,' he said,
    'For love did not find me
Upon the poisoned field of war
    Or on the sea,
And she will hold me in her arms
    Search with a tender eye,
That my cleft heart again be one
    And my wounds dry.'

[1] loth.
[2] before.
[3] above.
[4] e're, ever.

[5] combs.
[6] over, half way over.
[7] on the north shore of the Firth of Forth.

Long, long he rode the snapping brake
    Under a roof of spray,
And long I heard his bugle-horn
    At close of day,
Until the trees with leopard leaves
    Sprang softly into flame,
Ice silenced the loud waterfall
    And the snows came.

But when the fingers of the spring
    Had felt the dark earth through,
I met him by the forest oak
    In garments new.
As white as Sunday was his hair,
    His skin a wand new-peeled,
He bore no sword at his right hand,
    His wounds were healed.

'As through the heart's weather you rode,
    Prince, did you find your bride?'
The young man raised a sultry eye
    As he replied,
'I met my love as I was told
    Beneath the elder-tree,
But hers was not the face or form
    Long promised me.

'She lay upon the bridle-path,
    She gleamed upon a log,
Her eyes were two bold diamonds
    In a green frog,
And green and wet and wet and green
    To my cold hand she clung,
And crawled upon my murdered breast
    And kissed my tongue.

'She whispered to me as the sea,
    Entreated me to stay.
All things will change, she said, upon
    Our wedding day.
And so within my golden hand
    I hold the wedding-ring,
Sleep all night in a double-bed,
    And love is King.'

'Prince, when the forward morning through
  Your marriage window shone,
The white stars melting in the sky,
  The guests long gone,
You found that from your side the frog
  Had vanished like spring snow?
And in its place a loving bride?'

  'I do not know.'

CHARLES CAUSLEY

The Gypsy Countess

There came an earl a riding by,
A gypsy maid espied he.
O nut brown maid, to her he said,
I prithee come away with me.

I'll take you up, I'll carry you home,
I'll put a safe-guard over you,
Your shoes shall be of the Spanish leather,
And silken stockings all of blue.

My brothers three no more I'll see
If that I went along with you.
I'd rather be torn by thistle and thorn
With my bare feet all in the dew.

I'll lock you up in a castle tall,
I'll bar you up in a room so high,
Thou gipsy maid from greenwood glade,
That ne'er a gipsy shall come by.

Thou shalt no more be set in stocks
And trudge about from town to town,
But thou shalt ride in pomp and pride
In velvet red and broidered gown.

I'll pawn my hat, I'll pawn my gown,
I'll pawn my ribbons, stockings blue.
I'll pawn my petticoat next my shift
To follow along with the gypsies O!

All night you lie 'neath the starry sky,
In rain and snow you walk all day,

But ne'er thy head shall have feather bed
And in thy arms no husband lay.

I love to lie 'neath a starry sky,
I do not heed the rain and snow,
And I will away, come night come day,
To follow along with my gypsies O!

I will thee wed, sweet maid, he said,
I will thee wed with a golden ring,
Then you shalt dance and merry, merry be
And I'll make thee a gay wedding.

I will not wed, kind sir, she said,
I will not wed with a golden ring,
For fickle as wind I fear I'll find
The man that would make my wedding.

Three gypsies stood at the castle gate,
They sang so high, they sang so low.
The lady sat in her chamber late,
Her heart it melted away as snow.

They sang so sweet, they sang so shrill
That fast her tears began to flow
And she laid down her golden gown,
Her golden rings and all her show.

And she put off her silken shoes
That were of Spanish leather O
All forth for to go in the rain and snow,
All forth in the stormy weather,
And down the stair came the lady fair
To go away with the gypsies O.

At past midnight her lord came home
And where his lady was would know.
All servants replied on every side,
She's gone away with the gypsies O.

Come saddle my horse, come saddle my mare
And hang my sword to my saddle bow.
That I may ride for to seek my bride
That is gone away with the gypsies O.

They saddled his horse, they saddled his mare
And hung his sword on his saddle bow

That he might ride for to seek his bride
That was gone away with the gypsies O.

Then he rode high, then he rode low,
He rode through hills and valleys O,
He rode till he spied his own fair bride
Following along with the gypsies O.

What makes you leave both house and lands,
What makes you leave your money O,
What takes you abroad from your wedded lord
To follow along with the gypsies O?

O I want none of your house and lands
And I want none of your money O,
Neither care I for my wedded lord,
I will follow along with the gypsies O.

Last night you slept in a feather bed
Rolled in the arms of your husband O
And now you must sleep on the cold, cold ground
And walk along in the rain and snow.

I care not to sleep in a feather bed
Rolled in the arms of a husband O,
For rather I'd sleep on the cold, cold ground
And walk along in the rain and snow.

Nay, that shall not be, I swear, said he.
He drew his sword from his saddle bow,
And once he smote on her lily-white throat
And then her red blood down did flow.

ANON

CREATURES

The Squirrel's Nest

One day, when all the woods were bare and blea,[1]
I wandered out to take a pleasant walk
And saw a strange-formed nest on stoven tree
Where startled pigeon buzzed from bouncing hawk.

[1] Pale.

I wondered strangely what the nest could be
And thought besure it was some foreign bird,
So up I scrambled in the highest glee,
And my heart jumped at every thing that stirred.
'Twas oval-shaped; strange wonder filled my breast;
I hoped to catch the old one on her nest
When something bolted out – I turned to see –
And a brown squirrel pattered up the tree.
'Twas lined with moss and leaves, compact and strong;
I sluthered down and wondering went along.

JOHN CLARE

Emmonsails Heath in Winter

I love to see the old heaths withered brake
Mingle its crimpled[1] leaves with furze and ling
While the old heron from the lonely lake
Starts slow and flaps his melancholly wing

[1] Wrinkled, crumpled.

And oddling[1] crow in idle motion swing
On the half rotten ash trees topmost twig
Beside whose trunk the gipsey makes his bed
Up flies the bouncing woodcock from the brig[2]
Where a black quagmire quakes beneath the tread
The field fare chatter in the whistling thorn
And for the awe[3] round fields and closen[4] rove
And coy bumbarrels[5] twenty in a drove
Flit down the hedge rows in the frozen plain
And hang on little twigs and start again.

JOHN CLARE

The Meadow Mouse
I

In a shoe-box stuffed in an old nylon stocking
Sleeps the baby mouse I found in the meadow,
Where he trembled and shook beneath a stick
Till I caught him up by the tail and brought him in,
Cradled in my hand,
A little quaker, the whole body of him trembling,
His absurd whiskers sticking out like a cartoon-mouse,
His feet like small leaves,
Little lizard-feet,
Whitish and spread wide when he tried to struggle away,
Wriggling like a miniscule puppy.

Now he's eaten his three kinds of cheese and drunk from
    his bottle-cap watering-trough –
So much he just lies in one corner,
His tail curled under him, his belly big
As his head; his bat-like ears
Twitching, tilting toward the least sound.

Do I imagine he no longer trembles
When I come close to him?
He seems no longer to tremble.

---

[1] The odd one out; one differing from the rest of a family, brood or litter; generally applied to the smallest, or to one with a peculiarity.
[2] Variant of bridge.
[3] Variant of haw.   Whole line means: 'And rove around the enclosed fields
[4] Plural from of close.   looking for haws' (hawthorn berries).
[5] Long-tailed tits.

2

But this morning the shoe-box house on the back porch is
  empty.
Where has he gone, my meadow mouse,
My thumb of a child that nuzzled in my palm? –
To run under the hawk's wing,
Under the eye of the great owl watching from the elm-tree,
To live by courtesy of the shrike, the snake, the tom-cat.

I think of the nestling fallen into the deep grass,
The turtle gasping in the dusty rubble of the highway,
The paralytic stunned in the tub, and the water rising, –
All things innocent, hapless, forsaken.

THEODORE ROETHKE

Bats

A bat is born
Naked and blind and pale.
His mother makes a pocket of her tail
And catches him. He clings to her long fur
By his thumbs and toes and teeth.
And then the mother dances through the night
Doubling and looping, soaring, somersaulting –
Her baby hangs on underneath.
All night, in happiness, she hunts and flics.
Her high sharp cries
Like shining needlepoints of sound
Go out into the night and, echoing back,
Tell her what they have touched.
She hears how far it is, how big it is,
Which way it's going:
She lives by hearing.
The mother eats the moths and gnats she catches
In full flight; in full flight
The mother drinks the water of the pond
She skims across. Her baby hangs on tight.
Her baby drinks the milk she makes him
In moonlight or starlight, in mid-air.
Their single shadow, printed on the moon
Or fluttering across the stars,
Whirls on all night; at daybreak
The tired mother flaps home to her rafter.
The others all are there.
They hang themselves up by their toes,
They wrap themselves in their brown wings.
Bunched upside-down, they sleep in air.
Their sharp ears, their sharp teeth, their quick sharp faces
Are dull and slow and mild.
All the bright day, as the mother sleeps,
She folds her wings about her sleeping child.

RANDALL JARRELL

The Doll's-House Garden

This doll's-house garden was a magic land, a forest of flowers through which roamed creatures I had never seen before. Among the thick, silky petals of each rose-bloom lived tiny, crab-like spiders that scuttled sideways when disturbed. Their small, translucent bodies were coloured to match the flowers they inhabited: pink, ivory, wine-red, or buttery-yellow. On the rose-stems, encrusted with green flies, lady-birds moved like newly painted toys; lady-birds pale red with large black spots; lady-birds apple red with brown spots; lady-birds orange with grey-and-black freckles. Rotund and amiable, they prowled and fed among the anaemic flocks of greenfly. Carpenter bees, like furry electric-blue bears, zig-zagged among the flowers, growling fatly and busily. Humming-bird hawk moths, sleek and neat, whipped up and down the paths with a fussy efficiency, pausing occasionally on speed-misty wings to lower a slender proboscis into a bloom. Among the white cobbles large black ants staggered and gesticulated in groups round strange trophies: a dead cater-pillar, a piece of rose-petal, or dried grass-head fat with seeds. As an accompaniment to all this activity there came from the olive-groves outside the fuchsia hedge the incessant shimmering cries of the cicadas. If the curious, blurring heat-haze produced a sound, it would be exactly the strange chiming of these insects.

At first I was so bewildered by this profusion of life on our very doorstep that I could only move about the garden in a daze, watching now this creature, now that, constantly having my attention distracted by the flights of brilliant butterflies that drifted over the hedge. Gradually, as I became more used to the bustle of insect life among the flowers, I found I could concentrate more. I would spend hours squatting on my heels or lying on my stomach watching the private lives of the creatures around me, while Roger sat nearby, a look of resignation on his face. In this way I learnt a lot of fascinating things.

I found that the little crab-spiders could change colour just as successfully as any chameleon. Take a spider from a wine-red rose, where he had been sitting like a bead of coral, and place him in the depths of a cool white rose. If he stayed there – and most of them did – you would see his colour gradually ebb away, until, some two days later, he would be crouching among the white petals like a pearl.

I discovered that in the dry leaves under the fuchsia hedge lived another type of spider, a fierce little huntsman with the cunning and ferocity of a tiger. He would stalk about his continent of leaves, eyes glistening in the sun, pausing now and then to raise himself up on his hairy legs to peer about. If he saw a fly settle to enjoy a sun-bath he would freeze; then as slowly as a leaf growing, he would move forward, imperceptibly, edging nearer and nearer, pausing occasionally to fasten his life-line of silk to the surface of the leaves. Then, when close enough, the huntsman would pause, his legs shift minutely as he got a good purchase, and then he would leap, legs spread out in a hairy embrace, straight on to the dreaming fly. Never did I see one of these little spiders miss its kill, once it had manoeuvred into the right position.

All these discoveries filled me with a tremendous delight, so that they had to be shared, and I would burst suddenly into the house and startle the family with the news that the strange, spiky black caterpillars on the roses were not caterpillars at all, but the young of lady-birds, or with the equally astonishing news that the lacewing-flies laid eggs on stilts. This last miracle I was lucky enough to witness. I found a lacewing-fly on the roses and watched her as she climbed about the leaves, admiring her beautiful, fragile wings like green glass, and her enormous liquid golden eyes. Presently she stopped on the surface of a rose-leaf and lowered the tip of her abdomen. She remained like that for a moment and then raised her tail, and from it, to my astonishment, rose a slender thread, like a pale hair. Then, on the very tip of this stalk, appeared the egg. The female had a rest, and then repeated the performance until the surface of the rose-leaf looked as though it was covered with a forest of tiny club moss. The laying over, the female rippled her antennae briefly and flew off in a mist of green gauze wings.

GERALD DURRELL, *My Family and Other Animals*

Augustus

'I've got something for you,' said the old man at last, wiping his moustache carefully with a large red and white handkerchief. 'Another one of those terrible animals that you are so eager to get.'

Stuffing my mouth with the remains of the pop-corn and wiping my fingers on the grass, I asked him eagerly what it was.

'I'll fetch it,' he said, getting to his feet. 'It's a very curious thing. I've never seen one like it before.'

I waited impatiently while he went into the olive press and reappeared carrying a battered tin, the neck of which he had stuffed with leaves.

'There you are,' he said. 'Be careful, because it smells.'

I pulled out the plug of leaves, peered into the tin and discovered that Papa Demetrios was quite right, it smelt as strongly of garlic as a peasant bus on market day. In the bottom was crouched a medium size, rather smooth-skinned, greenish brown toad with enormous amber eyes and a mouth set in a perpetual, rather insane, grin. As I put my hand into the tin to pick him up, he ducked his head between his fore-

legs, retracted his protruberant eyes into his skull in the odd way that toads have and uttered a sharp bleating cry rather like that of a miniature sheep. I lifted him out of the tin and he struggled violently, exuding a terrible odour of garlic. I noticed that on each hind foot he had a horny black excrescence, blade-shaped, like a ploughshare. I was delighted with him for I had spent a considerable amount of time and energy trying to track down spade-footed toads without success. Thanking Papa Demetrios profusely, I carried him home triumphantly and installed him in an aquarium in my bedroom.

I had placed earth and sand to a depth of two or three inches at the bottom of the aquarium and Augustus, having been christened and released, immediately set to work to build himself a home. With a curious movement of his hind legs, working backwards, using the blades of his feet as spades, he very rapidly dug himself a hole and disappeared from view with the exception of his protruberant eyes and grinning face.

Augustus, I soon discovered, was a remarkably intelligent beast and had many endearing traits of character which made themselves apparent as he got tamer. When I went into the room, he would scuttle out of his hole and make desperate endeavours to reach me through the glass walls of the aquarium. If I took him out and placed him on the floor, he would hop round the room after me and then, if I sat down, would climb laboriously up my leg until he reached my lap, where he would recline in a variety of undignified attitudes, basking in the heat of my body, blinking his eyes slowly, grinning up at me and gulping. It was then that I discovered he liked to lie on his back and have his stomach gently massaged by my forefinger, and so from this unusual behaviour he derived the surname of Tickletummy. He would also, I learnt, sing for his food. If I held a large, writhing earth worm over the top of the aquarium, Augustus would go into paroxysms of delight, his eyes seeming to protrude more and more with excitement, and he would utter a series of little pig-like grunts and the strange bleating cry he had given when I first picked him up. When the worm was finally dropped in front of him, he would nod his head vigorously as if in thanks, grab one end of it and stuff it into his mouth with his thumbs. Whenever we had any guests, they were treated to an Augustus Tickletummy recital and they all agreed, gravely, that he had the best voice and repertoire of any toad they had met.

GERALD DURRELL, *Birds, Beasts and Relatives*

Hanno

Warmed by the coffee and bacon, Ping began to talk. It took his mind off the feeling that all was lost. It would also help to keep Mrs Oldknow's eyes off the garden. She was extremely interested to know what adventures had happened at Green Knowe in her absence. She listened and enjoyed Ping's crisp imaginative telling. He had reached an important event, when he became aware that she was not attending. Her eyes were directed over the top of his shoulder, and the sunlight that had been shining on him through the doorway was suddenly cut off. As he looked up, she said quietly:

'Don't move, Ping. Take no notice. Just go on as before. *He's here*. In the doorway.'

Her face was so lit up with excitement that the wrinkles seemed tensed away. She looked childlike, with that concentration of astonished curiosity that leaves no room for any other feeling.

Hanno stood resting his arm against the doorpost, his great head searching the room. He dwarfed the opening. He loomed like a natural force of the first order, causing the same thrill of recognition that a bather gives to an immense wave that has pulled up out of the ocean and suddenly towers hissing over him. It was impossible to see Hanno without taking in at the same time the dominance of the equatorial sun, the frier of the earth. The weight of silence in a thousand miles of forest, the ruthless interchange of life and death, are a millennium without time.

All this precipitated itself into the room, taking, on all fours, a more familiar form of wildness.

The old lady neither moved nor spoke. She received the full impact of Hanno's eyes which combined the directness of a lion's stare with the interchange of a man's. He had sagaciously tested the atmosphere before entering a possible trap. Green Knowe smelled of stone, of flowers, of wood smoke, of coffee, but nothing of a zoo, and Ping was there eating.

Ping cast his eye over the table. He took a long loaf of plaited bread and held it out. It was taken like the torch in a relay race, and the startling visitor withdrew, pausing only to give Ping a word of command.

'I'm sorry,' said Ping to his hostess. 'I had to give him the biggest thing to keep him quiet for a bit. But I think he was looking for me. I'm afraid he will come back. Hadn't I better go to him?'

Ping's Protector

The old lady had lost her rosy colour and was growing frighteningly white, so that Ping checked himself and stayed with her.

'Now I think I understand everything,' she said faintly. 'Ping darling, the game is up. Think of all those people at the front. Something dreadful will happen. You must help the Keeper to get him safely home. Go and find the Keeper.[1] Tell *him*. Don't tell anyone else. There's no forest for Hanno, poor splendid thing. Only a tight little urban overbuilt England. Go now, Ping. It's the only thing you can do for him. I would go myself, but I can't trust my legs.'

Ping ran out at the other side of the house as near sobbing as he had ever been in his life. Was it to be he who in the end gave Hanno up? It was an impossible thing to do. Even if he agreed it was the only possible end, his body would not have obeyed him, his tongue would refuse to speak. He ran, looking for nothing but a place to weep.

Now it happened that while this commotion was engaging the eastern side of Green Knowe, on the other side in the next hamlet there had been a small domestic mishap. A cow had calved in the field during the storm of the evening before, and having had the pleasure of her calf for so many hours, was unwilling to part with it when the farmer and his boy came to take it away. She ran head down at them again and again, keeping between them and the calf. More men were brought, but having won the first skirmish her blood was up. She attacked again, bellowing high screeches, but was shouted at, whacked, danced in front of and hit on the face, belaboured from all sides, outwitted and separated from her calf, till at last she charged about quite beside herself, not knowing what she was doing. She broke away from her tormentors and galloped along the river path with high, mad, female moos. Ping, sent on an errand he couldn't do, with his heart contracted to a dry clutch of pain was in the garden only vaguely aware of shouting crowds jumping over the garden wall and jostling to get through the gate. He thought of them only as Hanno's pursuers, thought Hanno must have shown himself on that side and that the crowds were surging to watch the capture or be in at the death. The cow swerved in at the gate and came at its lunatic unnatural gallop across the lawns straight for him. Just in time he came to himself and ran for dear life towards

[1] The Head Keeper of the zoo from which Hanno had escaped.

the nearest shelter, into the inner garden towards the bole of the big yew tree, too out of breath to pick his feet up properly. He tripped over the yew roots and sprawled headlong in the gravel. He gave himself up and waited to feel the horn in his ribs. But out of the branches came a whirling thunderbolt, flung with a spitting snarl between him and the cow. She stopped in her tracks, head down, swaying and uncertain. Hanno took her by the horns, his shoulder muscles twitched, and he flipped her over on her back, her neck broken like a stick. He stood there roused and excited, ready for more, not wasting a second glance at the cow. What he did needed no confirmation.

Ping was still panting on the ground, blood flowing from his nose and arms when the farmer and his men all with sticks came round the dividing hedge in pursuit of the cow. When they saw who was standing waiting for them, they fled like starlings, but one had breath enough to shout – 'The boy! There's a boy! Save the boy! Major! Here!' From all round voices shouted 'The gorilla! He's got a boy. He's mauled a boy.' Major Blair appeared with his gun, urged by the pointing arms of those who fled. A tide of people retreated at full speed from the garden.

And now Hanno saw again, face to face, his well remembered enemy, the man who had killed his father and taken himself and his sister captive. His heart swelled with a fury that was like a great joy. He stood to avenge these wrongs. He was his own drummer, beating his passionate chest, his own herald with that roar so horrifying that it can never be described, presenting himself for single combat against all comers and this one in particular who was due to be torn limb from limb. He gave fair warning, but before he had launched his onslaught the unfair bullet tore at his heart. He put his hands to his breast and pitched face downwards on the ground. In less than a split second all that was Hanno had ceased to exist.

The Keeper, who had got there as if by instinct, but too late, now helped the Major to turn him over. He looked with grim sorrow at the thirteen-year-old forest face from which all savagery had gone. For a gorilla never looks so tragically human as in the moment of death. Ping looked too, but not for long. He went indoors to look for Mrs Oldknow. She had been upstairs at the front of the house, trying to make out what was going on. She had seen the cow charge across the garden, had

heard the shouts, the roar, the shot. And now she saw with
overwhelming relief and affection Ping walking with a
deliberate jauntiness towards her, his face set like a pale
pebble under its smear of blood, his eyes hard like stars in a
frost.
'He's dead,' he said clearly and too composedly. 'It's all
right. That is how much he didn't want to go back, I saw him
choose.'

LUCY M. BOSTON, A Stranger at Green Knowe

'Men have been in our woods and killed our badgers'

Men have been in our woods and killed our badgers. We have
found the mother and babies ripped to pieces by dogs. We
have found the sett dug out as well. The children have known
the badger for three years and were very proud and happy
when we saw they had four or five cubs this year. We children
are shocked, disgusted, and horrified that grown-up people,
who should set us an example, should kill and destroy these
beautiful and harmless animals. These men are not primitive
people who have to hunt for food. They call this destroying
of life a sport. We think they are people who have not got
enough good things to occupy themselves. We would want
you to put this in your paper so that the men who did it may
see how we feel about it, and this may save someone else's
badgers from the dreadful fright and pain ours had.

Anthony Phillips (age 10), Michael Hewitt (10), Nicholas
Wilsdon (11), John Plested (9), Geoffrey Seligman (11),
Iain Bratchie (9), Lise Svendsen (11). (We wrote this
ourselves and it is what we feel.) – From St Gorran School,
Manaccan.

This letter appeared recently in our local paper. The children
whose badgers were killed go to a rather special school. St
Gorran lies at the head of a creek on the Helford River – one
of the loveliest parts of Cornwall. You go down to it through
winding lanes, where trees and May blossom meet overhead
to make a green tunnel and where dark green water lies in
pools, drifted round with bluebells, at the heads of the creeks.
We've never had such a year for blossom.
St Gorran has only twenty-eight pupils; some of them

come from wealthy homes ('we've had the children of diplomats, doctors, foreign princes even . . .!') but many have been sent there by local authorities from different parts of the country. They are children taken into care who are either delicate or to whom life has been so difficult that a small unit with a relaxed atmosphere is what is felt to be needed to enable their bruised spirits to heal. Who pays fees and who doesn't is not discussed, and the children follow their lessons, look after their farm animals, learn sailing in the creek, and keep their own newspaper, in a spirit of complete equality.

Living in such a setting, they are all natural history enthusiasts, collecting flowers, bird-watching, and following the lives and habits of animals. The badger sett was discovered three years ago in the private woodland surrounding the school buildings and was a cause of great joy.

Badger-baiting still goes on in Cornwall, and you can find advertisements offering for sale 'terriers, proved badger-baiters.' It is a peculiar sport. The huntsmen dig the badger from the sett and then pull him out with a special pair of tongs. And then the animal, held by men, is ripped to pieces by the terriers. The St Gorran children found their badger, a repulsive mess of blood and fur, by its sett along with some of its cubs; but the others had vanished, possibly for training terriers. After the letter appeared, the corpse of the badger also disappeared.

Strange pagan tales persist about badgers here – of badgers killed on Easter Sunday, on the incoming tide, thrown on to midsummer bonfires. At one time I dismissed it all as fantasy in this day and age. But I have met people who swear this still goes on and who specify two particular villages. It is unlikely, though, that one would ever discover the truth.

However, the result of that particular night's work is liable to have repercussions. A Devon woman, Mrs Ruth Murray, who is writing a book on badgers, wants to use this incident as a test case'to persuade the Government to make the badger a protected species. Some farmers say the badger is a pest, but its supporters swear it is harmless and both the Ministry of Agriculture and the Forestry Commission agree. The St Gorran children want to raise the money to offer a reward of £25 for information leading to the prosecution of the sportsmen involved. The league against Cruel Sports has actually offered £100 for such information.

The damage to these children's faith in adults, so pains-takingly being built up, is likely to take longer to repair. Life has already dealt enough suffering to some of these children. It is pitiful that in this idyllic place, full of the scents and sounds of summer, they should go out to pick flowers and find death at its nastiest.

JUDITH COOK from *The Guardian*

The Cock-Fight

Our wandering eyes are sated with the dancer's skill,
Our ears are weary with the sound of 'kung' and 'shang'[1].
Our host is silent and sits doing nothing:
All the guests go on to places of amusement.

On long benches the sportsmen sit ranged
Round a cleared room, watching the fighting-cocks.
The gallant birds are all in battle-trim:
They raise their tails and flap defiantly.
Their beating wings stir the calm air:
Their angry eyes gleam with a red light.
Where their beaks have struck, the fine feathers are
      scattered:
With their strong talons they wound again and again.
Their long cries enter the blue clouds;
Their flapping wings tirelessly beat and throb.
'Pray God the lamp-oil lasts a little longer,
Then I shall not leave without winning the match!'

TS'AO CHIH (A.D. 192–233), translated ARTHUR WALEY

The Darlaston Dog Fight

Down Sewerage Street where the smell ain't so sweet
Rough Moey flopped down on his flat-bottomed feet,
And under his arm The Pride of 'Em All,
The bitch as could bite a bolt hole through a wall.

And back of the Bull Stake by Darlaston Green,
Ben Bates brought his bitch, the Willenhall Queen;
The Queen had a mouth like a shark with the yaws[2],
And God help the dog as got stuck in her jaws.

[1] Notes of the scale.
[2] Contagious disease of the skin.

At scratch on the sewer a hundred were stood,
They'd all backed their fancy and thirsted for blood.
They backed with the bookie each bitch at odds on,
No matter who lost, he knew he had won.

The lickers[1] licked hard and they licked very well,
They dain't miss a hair on them dogs – you can tell;
A tot or two more and instead of a dog
They'd have licked all the spikes on a spavined[2] hedgehog.

Old Reuben was made referee of the match.
The Pride and The Queen was brought up to scratch,
The bell for the start the timekeeper smote,
And both of them dogs went for each other's throat.

The Queen missed The Pride and Ben Bates shed a tear,
The Pride missed The Queen with a snap you could hear.
Five minutes went by with no sign of a bite,
It was more like a dance than a fighting dog fight.

Rough cussed for a coward The Pride of 'Em All,
The Pride seemed too drunk to be bothered at all.
And as for The Queen, Ben Bates hung his head,
And cried to the crowd to say prayers for the dead.

Then into the pit jumped Rough Mo' with a roar,
He fell on his face and lay flat on the floor,
And then he found out why them dogs wouldn't bite:
Sewer gas in the pit: they was too drugged to fight.

Rough Mo' had a lungful and didn't feel too well,
He bit at them dogs – they bit back, you can tell,
The Queen had a bite that took half of his ear,
The Pride had a mouthful of ham off his rear.

No matter how Rough urged them dogs on to fight,
They both was too drugged and too beggared to bite.
He licked at The Queen which collapsed on the floor,
And she kicked at Rough where his backside was sore.

Them dogs at each other could not point a paw,
And Reuben declared that the match was a draw.
The bookmaker blarted[3] – he had to pay back
The money he thought was his own in the sack.

---

[1] Grooms.
[2] Having bony swellings.   [3] Cried.

That fight was the last by Ben Bates and his Queen,
Broken-hearted they died in the pub by the Green;
Rough Moey has never been able to sit
The same as afore he got bit in the pit.

TRADITIONAL

Fish

I have waited with a long rod
And suddenly pulled a gold-and-greenish, lucent fish from
  below,
And had him fly like a halo round my head,
Lunging in the air on the line.

Unhooked his gorping, water-horny mouth,
And seen his horror-tilted eye,
His red-gold, water-precious, mirror-flat bright eye;
And felt him beat in my hand, with his mucous, leaping
  life-throb.

D. H. LAWRENCE

THE WILD WEST

The Old-Time Cowhand

(i)

There's an old sayin' that 'a cowboy's a man with guts and a
hoss', and that's bout as good a definition as anyone could give.
If he didn't have guts he wouldn't last long; if he didn't have
a hoss he couldn't be a cowboy. When one old cowhand described his breed, he said, 'Cowboys is noisy fellers with bow
legs and brass stomachs that rides hosses and hates any kind
of work they can't do on one.' . . .
  Fiction's made the cowboy the most romantic part of the
West. He may have been a dashin' two-gun individual on
paper, but he wasn't so on the range. No Westerner thought
of 'im as bein' a type or character, or anything at all unusual.
He certainly never thought of 'imself as bein' anything extra-

ordinary or heroic. He'd likely been born to the cow business
and had rode a runnin' iron for a hobbyhoss. He became a
cowman from the bootheels up.

Most people enjoy readin' a good Western novel, yet they
should realize that the true cowboy spent long, lonely months
on the range workin' cattle, and wasn't forever skally-hootin'
into town all spraddled out in fancy trappin's worth a couple
of year's wages, and performin' marvelous shootin' stunts
with a six-gun. His life was anything but the excitin' round of
pleasure and thrills pictured in most stories and movies. He
might crave action on the range, but when he hit town his
cravin' was mostly for ham and eggs and other truck he couldn't
get at the chuck wagon[1] . . .

[1] Wagon carrying food (chuck).

Sometimes the real cowhand did ride hard on the roundup or when at other work which made it necessary, but when he set across the range on his day's work at the ranch, he didn't spur and gallop his hoss. He went in a steady, ceaseless, choppy little trot that would tire out a tenderfoot to follow all day. This short trot was a natural gait for the cow hoss, and he'd maintain it for a long time if not crowded too hard. The rider poked along completely relaxed to save both 'imself and his hoss . . .

A self-respectin' cowhand would never be caught goin' far on foot. Even if he only had to go two or three hundred yards, he preferred to ketch and saddle a bronc rather than furnish that motive power 'imself. From the bunkhouse to the corral was quite a passear[1] for 'im. Most of 'em had forked a hoss so long that they straddled chairs instead of settin' like a human.

(ii)

I have been interested in the cowboy and his lingo for more than sixty years – way back, as the cowboy would say, since I was 'fryin' size'. My real interest probably started when Jim Houston, a typical Texas cowboy, told a group of other cowmen, into which I had poked my young ears, of the time he had a narrow escape from a cow on the prod while he was afoot in a branding pen:

'There's no love-light in that cow's eyes as she makes for me,' said Jim. 'I fogs it across that corral like I'm going to a dance, an' she's a-scratchin' the grease off my pants at ever' jump. Seein' I can't make the fence in time, Brazos Gowdy jumps down off the fence an' throws his hat in the old gal's face. Seein' a cowboy come apart in pieces like that makes her hesitate till I climb the fence without losin' anything more'n some confidence, a lot o' wind, and a little dignity. You can take it from me, a cow with a fresh-branded calf might be a mother, but she shore ain't no *lady* . . . .'

The real cowhand's typical day was anything but romantic. There was no romance in getting up at four o'clock in the morning, eating dust behind a trail herd, swimming muddy and turbulent rivers, nor in doctoring screw worms, pulling stupid cows from bog holes, sweating in the heat of summer, and freezing in the cold of winter.

If, when he got to town, after long months out in the brush,

[1] Step, passage, journey.

on the lone prairie, or on the long, long trail, the cowboy 'cut his wolf loose' and had a little fun, he could hardly be blamed. He was a robust animal, full of vinegar and pride, and generally came from venturesome ancestors.

The old-time cowhand lived in the saddle. He was strictly a riding man, and detested walking, even for short distances. A self-respecting cowhand would never be going far on foot. This is why he was mighty particular about a straight riding job. When he was out of work and rode to a new range seeking a job, he was careful to inquire about the outfit before he arrived. He didn't want to sign up with some little 'three-up' outfit that didn't own enough beef to hold a barbecue. On such an outfit there would be chores to do that were beneath his dignity, such as feeding, digging post-holes, or cutting stove wood, and the only place a cowhand could cut wood and not hurt his pride was at a line camp where it was chop wood or 'no eat'.

When he 'hit' a fenced ranch for a job, he hoped that all the fencing and cross fencing had been done and no more post holes needed to be dug. He didn't want to be caught on the blister end of no damned shovel. High-heeled boots weren't made for foot work, and he wouldn't be caught in low-heeled shoes. But he didn't shirk any duty as long as it could be done from horseback. He worked without complaint long hours through flood and drought, heat and cold, and dust and blizzard, never once thinking of his own discomfort if the cattle and the welfare of his hoss demanded his attention.

Fighting prairie fires, the dangers of stampedes, the loneliness of range riding, the discomforts of standing guard in the rain or sleet – none of these things seemed unusual if he could do them from the back of a horse. On the other hand, he didn't even want to open a gate unless he could lean over and do it from the saddle. His profession was born of necessity, and with it was born a tradition that he followed jealously until he became the most colourful and picturesque hired man ever known. About the only footwork he considered honourable was roping in the corral, or doing the branding.

A lot of sunshine put that squint in the old-timer's eyes, and a lot of prairie wind tanned his face. That ten-gallon hat and those fancy boots were not what made him look like a cowman. It was the elements, the corral dust, the horse smell, and the cow-camp chuck that branded him. He could go away from the cow country and dress in fancy society togs, and another cowman would still know him to be a cowman.

After the fences came, most of these old-timers were always bellyaching with a yearning to go somewhere where they could spread a loop without getting it caught on a fence post. Most of the real old-timers have now saddled a cloud and ridden into the Great Beyond, and their like will never be seen again.

RAMON ADAMS, from *The Old-Time Cowhand*

Andy Adams[1]

There have been thousands of Andy Adams
only Andy was one of the few who had the words.
'Our men were plainsmen and were at home
as long as they could see the North Star.'
They got his drift when he laughed:
'Blankets? Never use them. Sleep on your belly and cover it
with your back and get up with the birds in the
morning.
'Saddles? Every good cowman takes his saddle wherever he
goes though he may not have clothes enough to dust a
fiddle.'
They could ride long hours in rain and sleet dozing and
taking short sleeps in their saddles, resting to linger over
their morning coffee.
This breed of men gone to a last roundup?
They will be heard from.
They tell us now any Texas girl is worth marrying.
'No matter what happens, she has seen worse.'

CARL SANDBURG, from *The People, Yes*

[1] Andy Adams was born on an Indiana farm in 1859. When he grew up he wandered to Texas where he became a cowboy in the great cattle days of the 1880s working up the long trail drives from the Texas ranches to the Kansas railheads. After some year ranching became more and more of a business and less and less of an adventure, so Andy Adams quit the life and became a Colorado miner. In 1892 he settled in Colorado Springs. Nine years later, after writing some short stories he produced his first book, *The Log of a Cowboy*, 1903. It is generally considered the finest book on the trail life of the open-range cowboy, for it presents an unpretentious yet stirring picture of the cowboy's day-to-day existence. Short extracts from the book follow. Andy Adams died, unmarried, in 1935. See p. 55 for a map of the trail.

Equipment

For the trip each man was expected to furnish his own accoutrements. In saddles, we had the ordinary Texas make, the housings of which covered our mounts from withers to hips, and would weigh from thirty to forty pounds, bedecked with the latest in the way of trimmings and trappings. Our bridles were in keeping with the saddles, the reins as long as plough lines, while the bit was frequently ornamental and costly. The indispensable slicker, a greatcoat of oiled canvas, was ever at hand, securely tied to our cantle[1] strings. Spurs were a matter of taste. If a rider carried a quirt[2], he usually dispensed with spurs, though, when used, those with large, dull rowels were the make commonly chosen. In the matter of leggings, not over half our outfit had any, as a trail herd always kept in the open, and except for night herding they were too warm in summer. Our craft never used a cattle whip, but if emergency required, the loose end of a rope served instead, and was more humane.

ANDY ADAMS, *The Log of a Cowboy*

Incident (i)

Coyotes had been hanging around our camp for several days, and during the quiet hours of the night these scavengers of the plain had often ventured in near the wagon in search of scraps of meat or anything edible. Rod Wheat and Ash Borrowstone had made their beds down some distance from the wagon; the coyotes as they circled round the camp came near their bed, and in sniffing about awoke Borrowstone. There was no more danger of attack from these cowards than from field mice, but their presence annoyed Ash, and as he dared not shoot, he threw his boots at the varmints. Imagine his chagrin the next morning to find that one boot had landed among the banked embers of the camp-fire, and was burned to a crisp. It was looked upon as a capital joke by the outfit, as there was no telling when we would reach a store where he could secure another pair.

Incident (ii)

Each trip was a repetition of the former, with varying incident. Every hoof was over in less than two hours. On the last trip,

[1] Raised hind part of saddle, the hind bow.
[2] Riding whip.

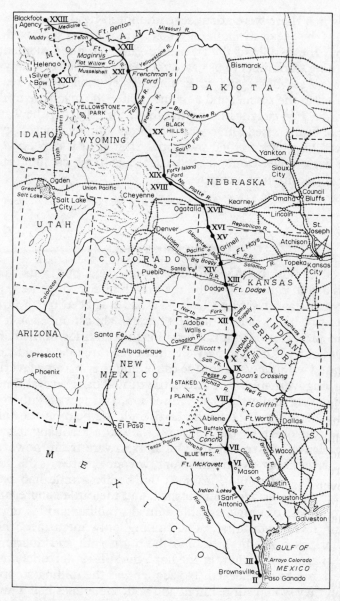

Map of the Trail

in which there were about seven hundred head, the horse of one of the Mexican vaqueros[1] took cramps, it was supposed, at about the middle of the river, and sank without a moment's warning. A number of us heard the man's terrified cry, only in time to see horse and rider sink. Every man within reach turned to the rescue, and a moment later the man rose to the surface. Fox caught him by the shirt, and, shaking the water out of him, turned him over to one of the other vaqueros, who towed him back to their own side. Strange as it may appear, the horse never came to the surface again, which supported the supposition of cramps.

ANDY ADAMS, *The Log of a Cowboy*

Cattle Blindness

Good cloudy weather would have saved us, but in its stead was a sultry morning without a breath of air, which bespoke another day of sizzling heat. We had not been on the trail over two hours before the heat became almost unbearable to man and beast. Had it not been for the condition of the herd, all might yet have gone well; but over three days had now elapsed without water for the cattle, and they became feverish and ungovernable. The lead cattle turned back several times, wandering aimlessly in any direction, and it was with considerable difficulty that the herd could be held on the trail. The rear overtook the lead, and the cattle gradually lost all semblance of a trail herd. Our horses were fresh, however, and after about two hours' work, we once more got the herd strung out in trailing fashion; but before a mile had been covered, the leaders again turned, and the cattle congregated into a mass of unmanageable animals, milling and lowing in their fever and thirst. The milling only intensified their sufferings from the heat, and the outfit split and quartered them again and again, in the hope that this unfortunate outbreak might be checked. No sooner was the milling stopped than they would surge hither and yon, sometimes half a mile, as ungovernable as the waves of an ocean. After wasting several hours in this manner, they finally turned back over the trail, and the utmost efforts of every man in the outfit failed to check them. We threw our ropes in their faces, and when this

[1]Herdsmen, cowboys.

failed, we resorted to shooting; but in defiance of the fusillade and the smoke they walked sullenly through the line of horsemen across their front. Six-shooters were discharged so close to the leaders' faces as to singe their hair, yet, under a noonday sun, they disregarded this and every other device to turn them, and passed wholly out of our control. In a number of instances wild steers deliberately walked against our horses, and then for the first time a fact dawned on us that chilled the marrow in our bones, – *the herd was going blind.*

The bones of men and animals that lie bleaching along the trails abundantly testify that this was not the first instance in which the plain had baffled the determination of man. It was now evident that nothing short of water would stop the herd, and we rode aside and let them pass. As the outfit turned back to the wagon, our foreman seemed dazed by the sudden and unexpected turn of affairs, but rallied and met the emergency.

'There's but one thing left to do,' said he, as we rode along, 'and that is to hurry the outfit back to Indian Lakes . . .'
. . . It was nearly noon the next day before the cattle began to arrive at the water holes in squads of from twenty to fifty. Pitiful objects as they were, it was a novelty to see them reach the water and slack their thirst. Wading out into the lakes until their sides were half covered, they would stand and low in a soft moaning voice, often for half an hour before attempting to drink. Contrary to our expectation, they drank very little at first, but stood in the water for hours. After coming out, they would lie down and rest for hours longer, and then drink again before attempting to graze, their thirst overpowering hunger. That they were blind there was no question, but with the causes that produced it once removed, it was probable their eyesight would gradually return.

ANDY ADAMS, *The Log of a Cowboy*

Prairie

I was born on the prairie, and the milk of its wheat, the red
    of its clover, the eyes of its women, gave me a song and
    a slogan.

Here the water went down, the icebergs slid with gravel,
    the gaps and the valleys hissed, and the black loam came,
    and the yellow sandy loam.

Here between the sheds of the Rocky Mountains and the
    Appalachians, here now a morning star fixes a fire sign over
    the timber claims and cow pastures, the corn belt, the
    cattle ranches.

Here the grey geese go five hundred miles and back with a

Here I know I will hanker after nothing so much as one
    more sunrise or a sky moon of fire doubled to a river
    moon of water.

The prairie sings to me in the forenoon and I know in the
    night I rest easy in the prairie arms, on the prairie heart.

After the sunburn of the day
handling a pitchfork at a hayrack,
after the eggs and biscuit and coffee,
the pearl-grey haystacks
in the gloaming
are cool prayers
to the harvest hands.

CARL SANDBURG

Slade

Slade was born in Illinois, of good parentage. At about
twenty-six years of age he killed a man in a quarrel and fled the
country. At St Joseph, Missouri, he joined one of the early
California-bound emigrant trains, and was given the post of
train master. One day on the plains he had an angry dispute
with one of his wagon drivers, and both drew their revolvers.
But the driver was the quicker artist, and had his weapon
cocked first. So Slade said it was a pity to waste life on so small
a matter, and proposed that the pistols be thrown on the
ground and the quarrel settled by a fist fight. The unsuspecting driver agreed, and threw down his pistol – whereupon
Slade laughed at his simplicity, and shot him dead!

He made his escape, and lived a wild life for a while, dividing his time between fighting Indians and avoiding an Illinois
sheriff, who had been sent to arrest him for his first murder. It
is said that in one Indian battle he killed three savages with his
own hand, and afterward cut their ears off and sent them, with
his compliments, to the chief of the tribe.

Slade soon gained a name for fearless resolution, and this
was sufficient merit to procure for him the important post of
overland division agent at Julesburg, in place of Mr Jules,
removed. For some time previously, the company's horses
had been frequently stolen, and the coaches delayed, by gangs
of outlaws, who were wont to laugh at the idea of any man's
having the temerity to resent such outrages. Slade resented
them promptly. The outlaws soon found that the new agent
was a man who did not fear anything that breathed the breath
of life. He made short work of all offenders. The result was
that delays ceased, the company's property was let alone, and
no matter what happened or who suffered, Slade's coaches
went through, every time! True, in order to bring about this
wholesome change, Slade had to kill several men – some say
three, others say four and others six – but the world was the
richer for their loss. The first prominent difficulty he had was
with the ex-agent Jules, who bore the reputation of being a
reckless and desperate man himself. Jules hated Slade for
supplanting him, and a good fair occasion for a fight was all he
was waiting for. By and by Slade dared to employ a man whom
Jules had once discharged. Next, Slade seized a team of stage
horses which he accused Jules of having driven off and hidden
somewhere for his own use. War was declared, and for a day
or two the two men walked warily about the streets, seeking
each other, Jules armed with a double-barreled shotgun, and
Slade with his history-creating revolver. Finally, as Slade
stepped into a store, Jules poured the contents of his gun into
him from behind the door. Slade was plucky, and Jules got
several bad pistol wounds in return. Then both men fell, and
were carried to their respective lodgings, both swearing that
better aim should do deadlier work next time. Both were bed-
ridden a long time, but Jules got on his feet first, and gathering
his possessions together, packed them on a couple of mules,
and fled to the Rocky Mountains to gather strength in safety
against the day of reckoning. For many months he was not
seen or heard of, and was gradually dropped out of the
remembrance of all save Slade himself. But Slade was not the
man to forget him. On the contrary, common report said that
Slade kept a reward standing for his capture, dead or alive!

After a while, seeing that Slade's energetic administration
had restored peace and order to one of the worst divisions of
the road, the overland stage company transferred him to the

Rocky Ridge division in the Rocky Mountains, to see if he
could perform a like miracle there. It was the very paradise of
outlaws and desperadoes. There was absolutely no semblance
of law there. Violence was the rule. Force was the only recog-
nized authority. The commonest misunderstandings were
settled on the spot with the revolver or the knife. Murders
were done in open day, and with sparkling frequency, and
nobody thought of inquiring into them. It was considered that
the parties who did the killing had their private reasons for it;
for other people to meddle would have been looked upon as
indelicate. After a murder, all that Rocky Mountain etiquette
required of a spectator was, that he should help the gentleman bury his game – otherwise his churlishness would surely
be remembered against him the first time he killed a man himself and needed a neighbourly turn in interring him.

Slade took up his residence sweetly and peacefully in the
midst of this hive of horse thieves and assassins, and the very
first time one of them aired his insolent swaggerings in his
presence he shot him dead! He began a raid on the outlaws,
and in a singularly short space of time he had completely
stopped their depredations on the stage stock, recovered a
large number of stolen horses, killed several of the worst
desperadoes of the district, and gained such a dread ascend-
ancy over the rest that they respected him, admired him,
feared him, obeyed him! He wrought the same marvelous
change in the ways of the community that had marked his
administration at Overland City. He captured two men who
had stolen overland stock, and with his own hands he hanged
them. He was supreme judge in his district, and he was jury
and executioner likewise – and not only in the case of offenses
against his employers, but against passing emigrants as well.
On one occasion some emigrants had their stock lost or
stolen, and told Slade, who chanced to visit their camp. With
a single companion he rode to a ranch, the owners of which he
suspected, and opening the door, commenced firing, killing
three, and wounding the fourth . . .

Slade was a matchless marksman with a navy revolver. The
legends say that one morning at Rocky Ridge, when he was
feeling comfortable, he saw a man approaching who had
offended him some days before – observe the fine memory
he had for matters like that – and, 'Gentlemen,' said Slade,
drawing, 'it is a good twenty-yard shot – I'll clip the third

button on his coat!' Which he did. The bystanders all admired it. And they all attended the funeral, too.

On one occasion a man who kept a little whiskey shelf at the station did something which angered Slade – and went and made his will. A day or two afterward Slade came in and called for some brandy. The man reached under the counter (ostensibly to get a bottle – possibly to get something else), but Slade smiled upon him that peculiarly bland and satisfied smile of his which the neighbours had long ago learned to recognize as a death warrant in disguise, and told him to 'none of that! – pass out the high-priced article.' So the poor barkeeper had to turn his back and get the high-priced brandy from the shelf; and when he faced around again he was looking into the muzzle of Slade's pistol. 'And the next instant,' added my informant, impressively, 'he was one of the deadest men that ever lived.'

The stage drivers and conductors told us that sometimes Slade would leave a hated enemy wholly unmolested, unnoticed, and unmentioned, for weeks together – had done it once or twice at any rate. And some said they believed he did it in order to lull the victims into unwatchfulness, so that he could get the advantage of them, and others said they believed he saved up an enemy that way, just as a schoolboy saves up a cake, and made the pleasure go as far as it would by gloating over the anticipation. One of these cases was that of a Frenchman who had offended Slade. To the surprise of everybody Slade did not kill him on the spot, but let him alone for a considerable time. Finally, however, he went to the Frenchman's house very late one night, knocked, and when his enemy opened the door, shot him dead – pushed the corpse inside the door with his foot, set the house on fire, and burned up the dead man, his widow and three children! I heard this story from several different people, and they evidently believed what they were saying. It may be true, and it may not. 'Give a dog a bad name,' etc.

Slade was captured, once, by a party of men who intended to lynch him. They disarmed him, and shut him up in a strong log house, and placed a guard over him. He prevailed on his captors to send for his wife, so that he might have a last interview with her. She was a brave, loving, spirited woman. She jumped on a horse and rode for life and death. When she arrived they let her in without searching her, and before the

door could be closed she whipped out a couple of revolvers,
and she and her lord marched forth defying the party.
And then, under a brisk fire, they mounted double and
galloped away unharmed!

In the fullness of time Slade's myrmidons captured his
ancient enemy Jules, whom they found in a well-chosen
hiding-place in the remote fastnesses of the mountains,
gaining a precarious livelihood with his rifle. They brought
him to Rocky Ridge, bound hand and foot, and deposited him
in the middle of the cattle yard with his back against a post. It
is said that the pleasure that lit Slade's face when he heard of
it was something fearful to contemplate. He examined his
enemy to see that he was securely tied, and then went to bed,
content to wait till morning before enjoying the luxury of
killing him. Jules spent the night in the cattle yard, and it is a
region where warm nights are never known. In the morning
Slade practised on him with his revolver, nipping the flesh
here and there, and occasionally clipping off a finger, while
Jules begged him to kill him outright and put him out of his
misery. Finally Slade reloaded, and walking up close to his
victim, made some characteristic remarks and then dispatched
him. The body lay there half a day, nobody venturing to touch
it without orders, and then Slade detailed a party and assisted
at the burial himself. But he first cut off the dead man's ears
and put them in his vest pocket, where he carried them for
some time with great satisfaction. That is the story as I have
frequently heard it told and seen it in print in California news-
papers. It is doubtless correct in all essential particulars . . .

Slade had been drunk and 'cutting up' all night. He and his
companions had made the town a perfect hell. In the morning,
J. M. Fox, the sheriff, met him, arrested him, took him into
court and commenced reading a warrant that he had for his
arrest, by way of arraignment. He became uncontrollably
furious, and *seizing the writ, he tore it up, threw it on the ground
and stamped on it.* The clicking of the locks of his companions'
revolvers was instantly heard, and a crisis was expected. The
sheriff did not attempt his retention; but being at least as
prudent as he was valiant, he succumbed, leaving Slade the
*master of the situation and the conqueror and the ruler of the
courts, law and law-makers.* This was a declaration of war, and
was so accepted. The Vigilance Committee now felt that the
question of social order and the preponderance of the law-

abiding citizens had then and there to be decided. They knew
the character of Slade, and they were well aware that they must
submit to his rule without murmur, or else that he must be
dealt with in such fashion as would prevent his being able to
wreak his vengeance on the committee, who could never
have hoped to live in the Territory secure from outrage or
death, and who could never leave it without encountering
his friends, whom his victory would have emboldened and
stimulated to a pitch that would have rendered them reckless
of consequences. The day previous he had ridden into Dorris's
store, and on being requested to leave, he drew his revolver
and threatened to kill the gentleman who spoke to him.
Another saloon he had led his horse into, and buying a bottle
of wine, he tried to make the animal drink it. This was not
considered an uncommon performance, as he had often
entered saloons and commenced firing at the lamps, causing a
wild stampede.

A leading member of the committee met Slade, and informed him in the quiet, earnest manner of one who feels the
importance of what he is saying: 'Slade, get your horse at
once, and go home, or there will be – to pay.' Slade started
and took a long look, with his dark and piercing eyes, at the
gentleman. 'What do you mean?' said he. 'You have no right
to ask me what I mean,' was the quiet reply, 'get your horse at
once, and remember what I tell you.' After a short pause he
promised to do so, and actually got into the saddle; but, being
still intoxicated, he began calling aloud to one after another of
his friends, and at last seemed to have forgotten the warning
he had received and became again uproarious, shouting the
name of a well-known courtesan in company with those of
two men whom he considered heads of the committee, as a
sort of challenge; perhaps, however, as a simple act of bravado.
It seems probable that the intimation of personal danger he
had received had not been forgotten entirely; though fatally
for him, he took a foolish way of showing his remembrance of
it. He sought out Alexander Davis, the Judge of the Court,
and drawing a cocked Derringer, he presented it at his head,
and told him that he should hold him as a hostage for his own
safety. As the judge stood perfectly quiet, and offered no
resistance to his captor, no further outrage followed on this
score. Previous to this, on account of the critical state of
affairs, the committee had met, and at last resolved to arrest

him. His execution had not been agreed upon, and, at that time, would have been negatived, most assuredly. A messenger rode down to Nevada to inform the leading men of what was on hand, as it was desirable to show that there was a feeling of unanimity on the subject, all along the gulch. The miners turned out almost *en masse*, leaving their work and forming in solid column. About six hundred strong, armed to the teeth, they marched up to Virginia. The leader of the body well knew the temper of his men on the subject. He spurred on ahead of them, and hastily calling a meeting of the executive, he told them plainly that the miners meant 'business', and that, if they came up, they would not stand in the street to be shot down by Slade's friends; but that they would take him and hang him. The meeting was small, as the Virginia men were loath to act at all. This momentous announcement of the feeling of the Lower Town was made to a cluster of men, who were deliberating behind a wagon, at the rear of a store on Main Street.

The committee were most unwilling to proceed to extremities. All the duty they had ever performed seemed as nothing to the task before them; but they had to decide, and that quickly. It was finally agreed that if the whole body of the miners were of the opinion that he should be hanged, that the committee left it in their hands to deal with him. Off, at hot speed, rode the leader of the Nevada men to join his command.

Slade had found out what was intended, and the news sobered him instantly. He went into P. S. Pfout's store, where Davis was, and apologized for his conduct, saying that he would take it all back.

The head of the column now wheeled into Wallace Street and marched up at quick time. Halting in front of the store, the executive officer of the committee stepped forward and arrested Slade, who was at once informed of his doom, and inquiry was made as to whether he had any business to settle. Several parties spoke to him on the subject; but to all such inquiries he turned a deaf ear, being entirely absorbed in the terrifying reflections on his own awful position. He never ceased his entreaties for life, and to see his dear wife. The unfortunate lady referred to, between whom and Slade there existed a warm affection, was at this time living at their ranch on the Madison. She was possessed of considerable personal attractions; tall, well-formed, of graceful carriage, pleasing manners, and was, withal, an accomplished horse-woman.

A messenger from Slade rode at full speed to inform her of her husband's arrest. In an instant she was in the saddle, and with all the energy that love and despair could lend to an ardent temperament and a strong physique, she urged her fleet charger over the twelve miles of rough and rocky ground that intervened between her and the object of her passionate devotion.

Meanwhile a party of volunteers had made the necessary preparations for the execution, in the valley traversed by the branch. Beneath the site of Pfout's and Russell's stone building there was a corral, the gate-posts of which were strong and high. Across the top was laid a beam, to which the rope was fastened, and a dry-goods box served for the platform. To this place Slade was marched, surrounded by a guard, composed of the best armed and most numerous force that has ever appeared in Montana Territory.

The doomed man had so exhausted himself by tears, prayers and lamentations, that he had scarcely strength left to stand under the fatal beam. He repeatedly exclaimed, 'My God! my God! must I die? Oh, my dear wife!'

On the return of the fatigue party, they encountered some friends of Slade, staunch and reliable citizens and members of the committee, but who were personally attached to the condemned. On hearing of his sentence, one of them, a stout-hearted man, pulled out his handkerchief and walked away, weeping like a child. Slade still begged to see his wife, most piteously, and it seemed hard to deny his request; but the bloody consequences that were sure to follow the inevitable attempt at a rescue, that her presence and entreaties would have certainly incited, forbade the granting of his request. Several gentlemen were sent for to see him, in his last moments, one of whom (Judge Davis) made a short address to the people; but in such low tones as to be inaudible, save to a few in his immediate vicinity. One of his friends, after exhausting his powers of entreaty, threw off his coat and declared that the prisoner could not be hanged until he himself was killed. A hundred guns were instantly levelled at him; whereupon he turned and fled; but, being brought back, he was compelled to resume his coat, and to give a promise of future peaceable demeanour.

Scarcely a leading man in Virginia could be found, though numbers of the citizens joined the ranks of the guard when the arrest was made. All lamented the stern necessity which dictated the execution.

Everything being ready, the command was given, 'Men, do your duty,' and the box being instantly slipped from beneath his feet, he died almost instantaneously.

The body was cut down and carried to the Virginia Hotel, where, in a darkened room, it was scarcely laid out when the unfortunate and bereaved companion of the deceased arrived, at headlong speed, to find that all was over, and that she was a widow. Her grief and heart-piercing cries were terrible evidences of the depth of her attachment for her lost husband, and a considerable period elapsed before she could regain the command of her excited feelings.

There is something about the desperado nature that is wholly unaccountable – at least it looks unaccountable. It is this. The true desperado is gifted with splendid courage, and yet he will take the most infamous advantage of his enemy; armed and free, he will stand up before a host and fight until he is shot all to pieces, and yet when he is under the gallows and helpless he will cry and plead like a child. Words are cheap, and it is easy to call Slade a coward (all executed men who do not 'die game' are promptly called cowards by un-reflecting people), and when we read of Slade that he 'had so exhausted himself by tears, prayers and lamentations, that he had scarcely strength left to stand under the fatal beam,' the disgraceful word suggests itself in a moment – yet in fre-quently defying and inviting the vengeance of banded Rocky Mountain cut-throats by shooting down their comrades and leaders and never offering to hide or fly, Slade showed that he was a man of peerless bravery. No coward would dare that. Many a notorious coward, many a chicken-livered poltroon, coarse, brutal, degraded, has made his dying speech without a quaver in his voice and been swung into eternity with what looked like the calmest fortitude, and so we are justified in believing, from the low intellect of such a creature, that it was not *moral* courage that enabled him to do it. Then, if moral courage is not the requisite quality, what could it have been that this stouthearted Slade lacked? – this bloody, desperate, kindly-mannered, urbane gentleman, who never hesitated to warn his most ruffianly enemies that he would kill them whenever or wherever he came across them next! I think it is a conundrum worth investigating.

MARK TWAIN, *Roughing It*

The Gun

It was plain that Shane was beginning to enjoy living with us and working the place. Little by little the tension in him was fading out. He was still alert and watchful, instinct with that unfailing awareness of everything about him. I came to realize that this was inherent in him, not learned or acquired, simply a part of his natural being. But the sharp extra edge of conscious alertness, almost of expectancy of some unknown trouble always waiting, was wearing away.

Yet why was he sometimes so strange and stricken in his own secret bitterness? Like the time I was playing with a gun Mr Grafton gave me, an old frontier model Colt with a cracked barrel someone had turned in at the store.

I had rigged a holster out of a torn chunk of oilcloth and a belt of rope. I was stalking around near the barn, whirling every few steps to pick off a skulking Indian, when I saw Shane watching me from the barn door. I stopped short, thinking of that beautiful gun under his bunk and afraid he would make fun of me and my sorry old broken pistol. Instead he looked gravely at me.

'How many you knocked over so far, Bob?'

Could I ever repay the man? My gun was a shining new weapon, my hand steady as a rock as I drew a bead on another one.

'That makes seven.'

'Indians or timber wolves?'

'Indians. Big ones.'

'Better leave a few for the other scouts,' he said, gently. 'It wouldn't do to make them jealous. And look here, Bob. You're not doing that quite right.'

He sat down on an upturned crate and beckoned me over. 'Your holster's too low. Don't let it drag full arm's length. Have it just below the hip, so the grip is about halfway between your wrist and elbow when the arm's hanging limp. You can take the gun then as your hand's coming up and there's still room to clear the holster without having to lift the gun too high.'

'Gosh agorry! Is that the way the real gunfighters do?'
A queer light flickered in his eyes and was gone. 'No. Not
all of them. Most have their own tricks. One likes a shoulder
holster; another packs a gun in his pants belt. Some carry two
guns, but that's a show-off stunt and a waste of weight. One's
enough, if you know how to use it. I've even seen a man have a
tight holster with an open end and fastened on a little swivel to
the belt. He didn't have to pull the gun then. Just swung up
the barrel and blazed away from the hip. That's mighty fast
for close work and a big target. But its not certain past ten or
fifteen paces and no good at all for putting your shot right
where you want it. The way I'm telling you is as good as any
and better than most. And another thing – '
He reached and took the gun. Suddenly, as for the first
time, I was aware of his hands. They were broad and strong,
but not heavy and fleshy like father's. The fingers were long
and square on the ends. It was funny how, touching the gun,
the hands seemed to have an intelligence all their own, a sure
movement that needed no guidance of thought.
His right hand closed around the grip and you knew at once
it was doing what it had been created for. He hefted the old
gun, letting it lie loosely in the hand. Then the fingers
tightened and the thumb toyed with the hammer, testing the
play of it.
While I gaped at him, he tossed it swiftly in the air and
caught it in his left hand and in the instant of catching, it
nestled snugly into his hand too. He tossed it again, high this
time, and spinning end over end, and as it came down, his
right hand flicked forward and took it. The forefinger slipped
through the trigger guard and the gun spun, coming up into
firing position in the one unbroken motion. With him that old
pistol seemed alive, not an inanimate and rusting metal object
but an extension of the man himself.
'If it's speed you're after, Bob, don't split the move into
parts. Don't pull, cock, aim, and fire. Slip back the hammer as
you bring the gun up and squeeze the trigger the second it's up
level.'
'How do you aim it, then? How do you get a sight on it?'
'No need to. Learn to hold it so the barrel's right in line
with the fingers if they were out straight. You won't have to
waste time bringing it high to take a sight. Just point it, low
and quick and easy, like pointing a finger.'

Like pointing a finger. As the words came, he was doing it.
The old gun was bearing on some target over by the corral and
the hammer was clicking at the empty cylinder. Then the
hand around the gun whitened and the fingers slowly opened
and the gun fell to the ground. The hand sank to his side,
stiff and awkward. He raised his head and the mouth was a
bitter gash in his face. His eyes were fastened on the mountains climbing in the distance.

'Shane! Shane! What's the matter?'

He did not hear me. He was back somewhere along the dark
trail of the past.

He took a deep breath, and I could see the effort run through
him as he dragged himself into the present and a realization of
a boy staring at him. He beckoned to me to pick up the gun.
When I did he leaned forward and spoke earnestly.

'Listen, Bob. A gun is just a tool. No better and no worse
than any other tool, a shovel – or an axe or a saddle or a stove
or anything. Think of it always that way. A gun is as good –
and as bad – as the man who carries it. Remember that.'

He stood up and strode off into the fields and I knew he
wanted to be alone. I remembered what he said all right,
tucked away unforgettably in my mind. But in those days I
remembered more the way he handled the gun and the advice
he gave me about using it. I would practise with it and think of
the time when I could have one that would really shoot.

And then the summer was over. School began again and the
days were growing shorter and the first cutting edge of cold
was creeping down from the mountains.

JACK SCHAEFER, *Shane*

A Soft Swish of Sound

Across the stunned and barren silence of the room Shane's
voice seemed to come from a great distance. 'I expect that
finishes it,' he said. Unconsciously, without looking down, he
broke out the cylinder of his gun and reloaded it. The stain on
his shirt was bigger now, spreading fanlike above the belt, but
he did not appear to know or care. Only his movements were
slow, retarded by an unutterable weariness. The hands were
sure and steady, but they moved slowly and the gun dropped
into the holster of its own weight.

He backed with dragging steps towards the swinging doors until his shoulders touched them. The light in his eyes was unsteady like the flickering of a candle guttering toward darkness. And then, as he stood there, a strange thing happened. How could one describe it, the change that came over him? Out of the mysterious resources of his will the vitality came. It came creeping, a tide of strength that crept through him and fought and shook off the weakness. It shone in his eyes and they were alive again and alert. It welled up in him, sending that familiar power surging through him again until it was singing again in every vibrant line of him.

He faced that room full of men and read them all with the one sweeping glance and spoke to them in that gentle voice with that quiet, inflexible quality.

'I'll be riding on now. And there's not a one of you that will follow.'

He turned his back on them in the indifference of absolute knowledge they would do as he said. Straight and superb, he was silhouetted against the doors and the patch of night above them. The next moment they were closing with a soft swish of sound.

JACK SCHAEFER, *Shane*

America's St Bartholomew

In June 1864,[1] after three uneasy years of non-compliance, Black Kettle and his band of some five hundred Cheyennes moved down to Sand Creek and encamped peaceably under a flag of truce. They had decided to resist the proclamation of the Territorial governor no longer. Here they were attacked by the paranoiac 'Colonel' J. M. Chivington (by profession a minister of religion!) and his blood-lusting Colorado militia men – who had been urged by their superior officers to spare neither man, woman nor child – and at least half of them massacred in cold blood. About two hundred Indian women and children and seventy men were slaughtered. Casualties among Chivington's 'boys' were negligible, but the consequences for the history of Indian-White relations and for the reputation of the white man in the West were to be momentous.

[1] By a treaty of 1861 the Cheyennes had been ordered on to a new reservation in the Sand Creek valley of south-eastern Colorado.

After more than a hundred years 'the Chivington Massacre' continues to be spoken and written about in tones of horror and incredulity. It is America's St Bartholomew.[1]

J. A. HAWGOOD, *The American West*

Settlement

Ten difficult years of Indian warfare which spanned the period between the Fetterman massacre[2] and Custer's defeat at the Little Bighorn[3] witnessed no other reverses comparable to these for the United States Army in the West. The transcontinental railroads split the buffalo herds of the plains and first the southern and then the northern herds were exterminated. The Plains Indians, deprived of the main basis of their economy – in part by the 'buffalo hunters' for the commercial value of the hides and the bones, partly as a deliberate policy of starving out the Indians – gradually let themselves be hounded into reservations, as 'wards' or pensioners of the Government, there to attempt to settle down to agriculture or cattle-ranching, if they turned their hands to anything at all. Those who continued to put up even a token resistance were only the most resolute, the most untameable and the ones possessing outstanding leaders. This was the age of the last generation of great Indian heroes.

J. A. HAWGOOD, *The American West*

Buffalo Dusk

The buffaloes are gone.
And those who saw the buffaloes are gone.
Those who saw the buffaloes by thousands and how they
    pawed the prairie sod into dust with their hoofs, their

---

[1] The name, the Massacre of St Bartholomew, was given to the massacre of Huguenots (French Protestants) which commenced in Paris on St Bartholomew's Day, 24 August 1572, and spread through the provinces during the succeeding weeks. The total number of those killed has been variously estimated at figures ranging from 5,000 to 70,000.
[2] It was near Fort Phil Kearney in December 1866 that Lieutenant-Colonel Fetterman and his whole force of eighty-one men were wiped out by a much larger band of Sioux, led by Crazy Horse.
[3] Scene of the 'last stand' 1876, near the Yellowstone River, Montana.

great heads down pawing on in a great pageant of dusk.
Those who saw the buffaloes are gone.
And the buffaloes are gone.

CARL SANDBURG

THE SENSES

Mark Twain's Boyhood

I spent some part of every year at the farm until I was twelve
or thirteen years old. The life which I led there with my
cousins was full of charm, and so is the memory of it yet. I can
call back the solemn twilight and mystery of the deep woods,
the earthy smells, the faint odours of the wild flowers, the
sheen of rain-washed foliage, the rattling clatter of drops
when the wind shook the trees, the far-off hammering of
woodpeckers and the muffled drumming of wood pheasants in
the remoteness of the forest, the snapshot glimpses of disturbed wild creatures scurrying through the grass – I can call
it all back and make it as real as it ever was, and as blessed. I
can call back the prairie, and its loneliness and peace, and a
vast hawk hanging motionless in the sky, with his wings
spread wide and the blue of the vault showing through the
fringe of their end-feathers. I can see the woods in their
autumn dress, the oaks purple, the hickories washed with gold,
the maples and the sumachs[1] luminous with crimson fires, and
I can hear the rustle made by the fallen leaves as we plowed
through them. I can see the blue clusters of wild grapes
hanging among the foliage of the saplings, and I remember
the taste of them and the smell. I know how the wild blackberries looked, and how they tasted, and the same with the
paw-paws,[2] the hazelnuts, and the persimmons[3]; and I can
feel the thumping rain, upon my head, of hickory[4] nuts and
walnuts when we were out in the frosty dawn to scramble for

[1] Kind of shrub or small tree.
[2] Fruit of South American tree.
[3] Date plums.
[4] Tree of walnut family.

them with the pigs, and the gusts of wind loosed them and sent them down. I know the stain of blackberries, and how pretty it is, and I know the stain of walnut hulls, and how little it minds soap and water, also what grudged experience it had of either of them. I know the taste of maple sap, and when to gather it, and how to arrange the troughs and the delivery tubes, and how to boil down the juice, and how to hook the sugar after it is made, also how much better hooked sugar tastes than any that is honestly come by, let bigots say what they will. I know how a prize watermelon looks when it is sunning its fat rotundity among pumpkin vines and 'simblins'; I know how to tell when it is ripe without 'plugging' it; I know how inviting it looks when it is cooling itself in a tub of water under the bed, waiting; I know how it looks when it lies on the table in the sheltered great floor space between house and kitchen, and the children gathered for the sacrifice and their mouths watering; I know the crackling sound it makes when the carving knife enters its end, and I can see the split fly along in front of the blade as the knife cleaves its way to the other end; I can see its halves fall apart and display the rich red meat and the black seeds, and the heart standing up, a luxury fit for the elect; I know how a boy looks behind a yardlong slice of that melon, and I know how he feels; for I have been there. I know the taste of the watermelon which has been honestly come by, and I know the taste of the watermelon which has been acquired by art. Both taste good, but the experienced know which tastes best. I know the look of green apples and peaches and pears on the trees, and I know how entertaining they are when they are inside of a person. I know how ripe ones look when they are piled in pyramids under the trees, and how pretty they are and how vivid their colours. I know how a frozen apple looks, in a barrel down cellar in the wintertime, and how hard it is to bite, and how the frost makes the teeth ache, and yet how good it is, notwithstanding. I know the disposition of elderly people to select the speckled apples for the children, and I once knew ways to beat the game. I know the look of an apple that is roasting and sizzling on a hearth on a winter's evening, and I know the comfort that comes of eating it hot, along with some sugar and a drench of cream. I know the delicate art and mystery of so cracking hickory nuts and walnuts on a flatiron with a hammer that the kernels will be delivered whole, and I know how the nuts, taken in conjunction with winter apples, cider, and doughnuts, make old people's old tales and old jokes sound fresh and crisp and enchanting, and juggle an evening away before you know what went with the time. I know the look of Uncle Dan'l's kitchen as it was on the privileged nights, when I was a child, and I can see the white and black children grouped on the hearth, with the firelight playing on their faces and the shadows flickering upon the walls, clear back toward the cavernous gloom of the rear, and I can hear Uncle Dan'l telling the immortal tales which Uncle Remus Harris was to gather into his books and charm the world with, by and by; and I can feel again the creepy joy which quivered through me when the time for the ghost story of the 'Golden Arm' was reached – and the sense of regret, too, which came over me, for it was always the last story of the evening and there was nothing between it and the unwelcome bed.

I can remember the bare wooden stairway in my uncle's house, and the turn to the left above the landing, and the rafters and the slanting roof over my bed, and the squares of moonlight on the floor, and the white cold world of snow outside, seen through the curtainless window. I can remember the howling of the wind and the quaking of the house on stormy nights, and how snug and cosy one felt, under the blankets, listening; and how the powdery snow used to sift in, around the sashes, and lie in little ridges on the floor and make the place look chilly in the morning and curb the wild desire to get up – in case there was any. I can remember how very dark that room was, in the dark of the moon, and how packed it was with ghostly stillness when one woke up by accident away in the night, and forgotten sins came flocking out of the secret chambers of the memory and wanted a hearing; and how ill chosen the time seemed for this kind of business; and how dismal was the hoo-hooing of the owl and the wailing of the wolf, sent mourning by on the night wind.

I remember the raging of the rain on that roof, summer nights, and how pleasant it was to lie and listen to it, and enjoy the white splendour of the lightning and the majestic booming and crashing of the thunder. It was a very satisfactory room, and there was a lightning rod which was reachable from the window, an adorable and skittish thing to climb up and down, summer nights, when there were duties on hand of a sort to make privacy desirable.

I remember the 'coon and 'possum hunts, nights, with the negroes, and the long marches through the black gloom of the woods, and the excitement which fired everybody when the distant bay of an experienced dog announced that the game was treed; then the wild scramblings and stumblings through briers and bushes and over roots to get to the spot; then the lighting of a fire and the felling of the tree, the joyful frenzy of the dogs and the negroes, and the weird picture it all made in the red glare – I remember it all well, and the delight that everyone got out of it, except the 'coon.

I remember the pigeon seasons, when the birds would come in millions and cover the trees and by their weight break down the branches. They were clubbed to death with sticks; guns were not necessary and were not used. I remember the squirrel hunts, and prairie-chicken hunts, and wild-turkey hunts, and all that; and how we turned out, mornings, while it was still dark, to go on these expeditions, and how chilly and dismal it was, and how often I regretted that I was well enough to go. A toot on a tin horn brought twice as many dogs as were needed, and in their happiness they raced and scampered about, and knocked small people down, and made no end of unnecessary noise. At the word, they vanished away toward the woods, and we drifted silently after them in the melancholy gloom. But presently the grey dawn stole over the world, the birds piped up, then the sun rose and poured light and comfort all around, everything was fresh and dewy and fragrant, and life was a boon again. After three hours of tramping we arrived back wholesomely tired, overladen with game, very hungry, and just in time for breakfast.

MARK TWAIN, *Autobiography*

Pleasant Sounds

The rustling of leaves under the feet in woods and under
    hedges;
The crumpling of cat-ice and snow down wood-rides,
    narrow lanes and every street causeway:
Rustling through a wood or rather rushing, while the wind
    halloos in the oak-top like thunder;
The rustle of birds' wings startled from their nests or
    flying unseen into the bushes;

The whizzing of larger birds overhead in a wood, such as
  crows, puddocks,[1] buzzards;
The trample of robins and woodlarks on the brown leaves,
  and the patter of squirrels on the green moss;
The fall of an acorn on the ground, the pattering of nuts on
  the hazel branches as they fall from ripeness;
The flirt of the groundlark's wing from the stubbles – how
  sweet such pictures on dewy mornings, when the dew
  flashes from its brown feathers!

                                              JOHN CLARE

New Corn

Swiftly the years, beyond recall.
Solemn the stillness of this fair morning.
I will clothe myself in spring-clothing
And visit the slopes of the Eastern Hill.
By the mountain-stream a mist hovers,
Hovers a moment, then scatters.
There comes a wind blowing from the south
That brushes the fields of new corn.

                     T'AO CH'IEN, translated ARTHUR WALEY

Winter Gold

The same gold of summer was on the winter hills,
the oat straw gold, the gold of slow sun change.

The stubble was chilly and lonesome,
the stub feet clomb up the hills and stood.

The flat cry of one wheeling crow faded and came,
ran on the stub gold flats and faded and came.

Fade-me, find-me, slow lights rang their changes
on the flats of oat straw gold on winter hills.

                                           CARL SANDBURG

[1] Fan-tailed, or fork-tailed kite.

The Shell

I

And then I pressed the shell
Close to my ear,
And listened well.

And straightway, like a bell,
Came low and clear
The slow, sad murmur of far distant seas

Whipped by an icy breeze
Upon a shore
Wind-swept and desolate.

It was a sunless strand that never bore
The footprint of a man,
Nor felt the weight

Since time began
Of any human quality or stir,
Save what the dreary winds and waves incur.

II

And in the hush of waters was the sound
Of pebbles, rolling round;
For ever rolling, with a hollow sound:

And bubbling sea-weeds, as the waters go,
Swish to and fro
Their long cold tentacles of slimy grey:

There was no day;
Nor ever came a night
Setting the stars alight

To wonder at the moon:
Was twilight only, and the frightened croon,
Smitten to whimpers, of the dreary wind

And waves that journeyed blind . . .
And then I loosed my ear – Oh, it was sweet
To hear a cart go jolting down the street.

JAMES STEPHENS

The Cowrie Shell

My own little sea is held in a shell.
When I put it to my ear

I hear the roar of the waves
Beating on the rocks.
I hear no gulls cry
Nor any happy shouts.
All I hear are the waves
Beating on the rocks.

YVONNE WILCOCK (*Aged 10*)

Country Sounds

I loved the scent and sound of the hay . . . the gentle rustling of
it past my ears as great masses were pitched to me by Poddy
and the bouncy softness which sometimes reassured me in my
dread of falling from the top of the load down the rutted track
to the stockyards. I would listen for the creaking of the stock-
yard gates as Poddy opened them to let in our hay-load; the
squelch of tumbril wheels on soiled and wetted straw which
would soon be ripe enough to enrich the soil for another
season's plantings; the moos of appreciation from the heifers
as they nuzzled at our load; the squeals and grunts from impatient pigs who had yet to be fed with pollard, swill and root-
crops; and the music from the tall trees and the roof of the
harness-room, where wheeled and squatted fan-tailed pigeons
and turtle doves in a harmony of cooings and love murmurs.
'One more load, then breakfast,' Poddy would say.

SPIKE MAYS, *Reuben's Corner*

Sunset

She went over the sheep-bridge and across a corner of the
meadow to the cricket-ground. The meadows seemed one
space of ripe, evening light, whispering with the distant mill-
race. She sat on a seat under the alders in the cricket-ground
and fronted the evening. Before her, level and solid, spread
the big green cricket-field, like the bed of a sea of light.
Children played in the bluish shadow of the pavilion. Many
rooks, high up, came cawing home across the softly-woven
sky. They stooped in a long curve down into the golden glow,
concentrating, cawing, wheeling, like black flakes on a slow
vortex, over a tree clump that made a dark boss among the
pasture.

A few gentlemen were practising, and Mrs Morel could hear the chock of the ball, and the voices of men suddenly roused; could see the white forms of men shifting silently over the green, upon which already the under-shadows were smouldering. Away at the grange, one side of the haystacks was lit up, the other sides blue-grey. A waggon of sheaves rocked small across the melting light.

The sun was going down. Every open evening, the hills of Derbyshire were blazed over with red sunset. Mrs Morel watched the sun sink from the glistening sky, leaving a soft flower-blue overhead, while the western space went red, as if all the fire had swum down there, leaving the bell cast flawless blue. The mountain-ash berries across the field stood fierily out from the dark leaves for a moment. A few shocks of corn in a corner of the fallow stood up as if alive; she imagined them bowing; perhaps her son would be a Joseph. In the east, a mirrored sunset floated pink opposite the west's scarlet. The big haystacks on the hillside, that butted into the glare, went cold.

D. H. LAWRENCE, *Sons and Lovers*

'Keep it a-pourin'!'

When corn canaried the fields at ripening time, the symphony of sounds was modulated as man-made notes dominated the scene – the scythe-swishings round the headlands as sweaty mowers cut avenues for horse-drawn reapers; the steely chatterings as triangular daggers raped the corn-stalks close to the soils; the clonkings as the mechanical reaper's fork paid out great sheaves in tidy lines ready for 'shocking'; the guiding calls from the driver to his horses . . . 'Gee, then, Boxer!' . . . 'Walkameller, Gipsy!'; the clinking of pint-pots; the gurglings from the neck of the wicker-encased earthenware jars as ale gushed forth from the two-gallon treasure for 'levenses; the shots from farmers' guns; yelps of delight from women, men and dogs, as hares and rabbits streaked in fear from the last few rods of uncut corn; the voices of the reapers themselves.

'Good owd yield. They sheaves are a-layin' tidy thick this year. Clean, too, nary a thistle, nary a dock.'

Later would be heard the rattling and rolling of wagons

across the stubble seas to net the golden corn and the shouts of
warning to the 'loader' from the boy horse-leader.

'Howd-ye-toight, howd-ye-toight! Whoah there, Boxer!'

Then, after celebration, the fruits would go to the miller.

There is a sadness in me that mill sails are now static,
silenced; no more does the western wind whisper through
rotating vanes; never again will be heard the great creaking of
wooden cogs or the grinding of flat circular stones to powder
the grain of wheat to nourishing flour; the voice of old Bragg,
the miller can no longer be heard:

'Thass roight, bor[1]. Le's hev another score o' sacks. Keep
the grain a-pourin', keep it a-pourin'!'

SPIKE MAYS, *Reuben's Corner*

Silence and Sun

One of our young school-teachers, with whom we children
were almost like friends, announced one day:

'Boys, I am going to take you to visit our village.'

We had heard that this village was at the foot of Mount
Mastar; that there were trees there, centuries old, in the trunks
of which whole families could be accommodated and where
they could live. We had also heard that from beneath the
village church water poured out with such abundance that it
could have carried away two whole carts, complete with the
oxen. Beside the village flowed the River Aradsany, like an
undulating blue ribbon.

We set off on foot in the evening to avoid the heat of the sun.
We went by short cuts, sometimes walking through golden
fields with the stars shining in the blue dome above. We
joked and playfully pushed and punched one another; we
drank from the clear, singing brooks, on the banks of which
the grass was of a fresh green.

We entered a cornfield which extended to infinity.

As we continued our way through it the sky became lower
and lower, and the stars gleamed down into our eyes. The
limpid silence was disturbed only by us and by the shooting-
stars.

'Shall we stop here until the morning star appears?' sug-
gested our teacher.

---

[1] Term of familiar address in the region of East Anglia. The word is the same as
the ending 'bour' in 'neighbour'.

And we stopped.
The silence became more still, the sky even lower.
We lay down in the corn.
The air was as pure and as clear as the waters of the brooks.
There was not a rustle to be heard anywhere. The only
audible sound was the breathing of my sleeping friends, and
that seemed like the whispering of the golden ears of corn . . .
I wanted everything to come to a standstill, just as it was
then: the sky with its stars, the earth with its corn, the silence
with its crystalline indigo . . .
A small white cloud, the size of a sheet, appeared from no-
where and began to sway in the lilac mist. It floated for a
while, became diffuse, and dissolved away like a dream. My
eyes were closing, but I waited for the morning star.
Suddenly, I heard my friends' voices. I opened my eyes:
the rising sun was bathing in the corn.
It roused new perfumes in the fields – the perfumes which
had lain dormant in the bosom of the night. And the colours,
too, awoke everywhere, as did the myriads of birds.
Everything came to life with the sun.

VAHAN TOTOVENTS, trans. MISCHA KUDIAN, *Scenes from an Armenian
Childhood*

The Balloons

Against these turbid turquoise skies
The light and luminous balloons
Dip and drift like satin moons,
Drift like silken butterflies;

Reel with every windy gust,
Rise and reel like dancing girls,
Float like strange transparent pearls,
Fall and float like silver dust.

OSCAR WILDE

Orchids

They lean over the path,
Adder-mouthed,
Swaying close to the face,
Coming out, soft and deceptive,

Limp and damp, delicate as a young bird's tongue;
Their fluttery fledgling lips
Move slowly,
Drawing in the warm air.

And at night,
The faint moon falling through whitewashed glass,
The heat going down
So their musky smell comes even stronger,
Drifting down from their mossy cradles:
So many devouring infants!
Soft luminescent finger,
Lips neither dead nor alive,
Loose ghostly mouths
Breathing.

THEODORE ROETHKE

MENU

Churning Day

A thick crust, coarse-grained as limestone, rough-cast,
hardened gradually on top of the four crocks
that stood, large pottery bombs, in the small pantry.
After the hot brewery of gland, cud and udder
cool porous earthenware fermented the buttermilk
for churning day, when the hooped churn was scoured
with plumping kettles and the busy scrubber
echoed daintily on the seasoned wood.
It stood then, purified, on the flagged kitchen floor.

Out came the four crocks, spilled their heavy lip
of cream, their white insides, into the sterile churn.
The staff, like a great whisky muddler[1] fashioned
in deal wood, was plunged in, the lid fitted.
My mother took first turn, set up rhythms
that slugged and thumped for hours. Arms ached.
Hands blistered. Cheeks and clothes were spattered
with flabby milk.

         Where finally gold flecks
began to dance. They poured hot water then,
sterilized a birchwood-bowl
and little corrugated butter-spades.
Their short stroke quickened, suddenly
a yellow curd was weighting the churned up white,
heavy and rich, coagulated sunlight
that they fished, dripping, in a wide tin strainer,
heaped up like gilded gravel in the bowl.

The house would stink long after churning day,
acrid as a sulphur mine. The empty crocks
were ranged along the wall again, the butter
in soft printed slabs was piled on pantry shelves.
And in the house we moved with gravid[2] ease,

---

[1] Churning stick.
[2] Bounteous, ample, abundant (literally, heavy with young).

our brains turned crystals full of clean deal churns,
the plash and gurgle of the sour-breathed milk,
the pat and slap of small spades on wet lumps.

SEAMUS HEANEY

A Meal

On the boil sure enough: a plume of steam from the spout.
He scalded and rinsed out the teapot and put in four full
spoons of tea, tilting the kettle then to let the water flow in.
Having set it to draw, he took off the kettle and crushed the pan
flat on the live coals and watched the lump of butter slide and
melt. While he unwrapped the kidney the cat mewed hungrily
against him. Give her too much meat and she won't mouse.
Say they won't eat pork. Kosher.[1] Here. He let the blood-
smeared paper fall to her and dropped the kidney amid the
sizzling butter sauce. Pepper. He sprinkled it through his
fingers, ringwise, from the chipped eggcup . . .
He prodded a fork into the kidney and slapped it over: then
fitted the teapot on the tray. Its hump bumped as he took it up.
Everything on it? Bread and butter, four, sugar, spoon, her
cream. Yes. He carried it upstairs, his thumb hooked in the
teapot handle.
Nudging the door open with his knee he carried the tray in
and set it on the chair by the bedhead.
– What a time you were, she said. . . .
The sluggish cream wound curdling spirals through her
tea. . . .
Her spoon ceased to stir up the sugar. She gazed straight
before her, inhaling through her arched nostrils.
– There's a smell of burn, she said. Did you leave anything
on the fire?
– The kidney! he cried suddenly.
He fitted the book roughly into his inner pocket and,
stubbing his toes against the broken commode, hurried out
towards the smell, stepping hastily down the stairs with a
flurried stork's legs. Pungent smoke shot up in an angry
jet from a side of the pan. By prodding a prong of the fork
under the kidney he detached it and turned it turtle on its
back. Only a little burned. He tossed it off the pan on to a
plate and let the scanty brown gravy trickle over it.

---

[1] Said of food, or of a shop where food is sold fulfilling requirements of Jewish law
and custom.

Cup of tea now. He sat down, cut and buttered a slice of the loaf. He shore away the burnt flesh and flung it to the cat. Then he put a forkful into his mouth, chewing with discernment the toothsome pliant meat. Done to a turn. A mouthful of tea. Then he cut away dies of bread, sopped one in the gravy and put it in his mouth. What was that about some young student and a picnic? He creased out the letter at his side, reading it slowly as he chewed, sopping another die of bread in the gravy and raising it to his mouth.

JAMES JOYCE, *Ulysses*

Cagliari Market

We went down the little street – but saw more baskets emerging from a broad flight of stone stairs, enclosed. So up we went – and found ourselves in the vegetable market. Here the q-b[1] was happier still. Peasant women, sometimes barefoot, sat in their tight little bodices and voluminous, coloured skirts behind the piles of vegetables, and never have I seen a lovelier show. The intense deep green of spinach seemed to predominate, and out of that came the monuments of curd-white and black-purple cauliflowers: but marvellous cauliflowers, like a flower show, the purple ones intense as great bunches of violets. From this green, white, and purple massing struck out the vivid rose-scarlet and blue-crimson of radishes, large radishes like little turnips in piles. Then the long, slim, grey-purple buds of artichokes, and dangling clusters of dates, and piles of sugar-dusty white figs and sombre-looking black figs, and bright burnt figs: basketfuls and basketfuls of figs. A few baskets of almonds, and many huge walnuts. Basket-pans of native raisins. Scarlet peppers like trumpets: magnificent fennels[2], so white and big and succulent: baskets of new potatoes: scaly kohlrabi[3]: wild asparagus in bunches, yellow-budding sparacelli[4]: big clean-fleshed carrots: feathery salads with white hearts: long, brown-purple onions and then, of course, pyramids of big oranges, pyramids of pale apples, and baskets of brilliant shiny mandarini, the little tangerine oranges with their green-

[1] q-b signifies 'queen-bee' which was Lawrence's pet-name here for his wife, Frieda.
[2] Fragrant herb.
[3] Kind of cabbage (with turnip-shaped stem).
[4] A kind of asparagus.

black leaves. The green and vivid-coloured world of fruit-gleams I have never seen in such splendour as under the market roof at Cagliari: so raw and gorgeous.

D. H. LAWRENCE, *Sea and Sardinia*

HOMES AND ENVIRONMENT

Early Morning at Home

He always made his own breakfast. Being a man who rose early and had plenty of time he did not, as some miners do, drag his wife out of bed at six o'clock. At five, sometimes earlier, he woke, got straight out of bed, and went downstairs. When she could not sleep, his wife lay waiting for this time, as for a period of peace. The only real rest seemed to be when he was out of the house.

He went downstairs in his shirt and then struggled into his pit-trousers, which were left on the hearth to warm all night.

There was always a fire, because Mrs Morel raked. And the
first sound in the house was the bang, bang of the poker
against the raker, as Morel smashed the remainder of the coal
to make the kettle, which was filled and left on the hob,
finally boil. His cup and knife and fork, all he wanted except
just the food, was laid ready on the table on a newspaper. Then
he got his breakfast, made the tea, packed the bottom of the
doors with rugs to shut out the draught, piled a big fire, and
sat down to an hour of joy. He toasted his bacon on a fork and
caught the drops of fat on his bread; then he put the rasher on
his thick slice of bread, and cut off chunks with a clasp-knife,
poured his tea into his saucer, and was happy. With his family
about, meals were never so pleasant. He loathed a fork: it is a
modern introduction which has still scarcely reached common
people. What Morel preferred was a clasp-knife. Then, in
solitude, he ate and drank, often sitting, in cold weather, on a
little stool with his back to the warm chimney-piece, his food
on the fender, his cup on the hearth. And then he read the last
night's newspaper – what he could – spelling it over laboriously. He preferred to keep the blinds down and the candle
lit even when it was daylight; it was the habit of the mine.

At a quarter to six he rose, cut two thick slices of bread and
butter, and put them in the white calico snap-bag. He filled his
tin bottle with tea. Cold tea without milk or sugar was the
drink he preferred for the pit. Then he pulled off his shirt, and
put on his pit-singlet, a vest of thick flannel cut low round the
neck, and with short sleeves like a chemise.

Then he went upstairs to his wife with a cup of tea because she was ill, and because it occurred to him.

'I've brought thee a cup o' tea, lass,' he said.

'Well, you needn't, for you know I don't like it,' she replied.

'Drink it up; it'll pop thee off to sleep again.'

She accepted the tea. It pleased him to see her take it and
sip it.

'I'll back my life there's no sugar in,' she said.

'Yi – there's one big un,' he replied, injured.

'It's a wonder,' she said sipping again.

She had a winsome face when her hair was loose. He loved
her to grumble at him in this manner. He looked at her again,
and went, without any sort of leave-taking. He never took
more than two slices of bread and butter to eat in the pit, so an
apple or an orange was a treat to him. He always liked it when

she put one out for him. He tied a scarf round his neck, put on his great, heavy boots, his coat, with the big pocket, that carried his snap-bag and his bottle of tea, and went forth into the fresh morning air, closing, without locking, the door behind him. He loved the early morning, and the walk across the fields. So he appeared at the pit-top, often with a stalk from the hedge between his teeth, which he chewed all day to keep his mouth moist, down the mine, feeling quite as happy as when he was in the field.

Later, when the time for the baby grew nearer, he would bustle round in his slovenly fashion, poking out the ashes, rubbing the fireplace, sweeping the house before he went to work. Then, feeling very self-righteous, he went upstairs.

'Now I'm cleaned up for thee: tha's no 'casions ter stir a peg all day, but sit and read thy books.'

Which made her laugh, in spite of her indignation.

'And the dinner cooks itself?' she answered.

'Eh, I know nowt about th' dinner.'

'You'd know if there weren't any.'

'Ay, 'appen so,' he answered, departing.

D. H. LAWRENCE, *Sons and Lovers*

'It's lovely and warm down there'

Cowed and shrinking, Alfie's nervous, propitiatory smile invited your sympathy. His father stayed in the pubs until closing time or until his money ran out. If the cupboard were empty, as it all too often was, Alfie had to fend for himself. My sister and I shared our toast, dripping and tea with him be-times. He also found a fish-and-chip shop proprietor who had charity in her heart. When, around eleven o'clock, the lady was about to close the shop he came out of the shadows, went to the counter and asked: 'Are there any scratchings, mam?' Scratchings was our name for the tiny globules of fat that accumulated in the bottom of the fryer. She scooped these into a paper together with any other leftovers and passed them to Alfie, who stood outside wolfing them. His signal to be home and abed was when 'Sweet Adeline', in tipsy harmony, announced the imminent return of his belted parent. If he were caught Alfie dodged the clumsily swung belt and disappeared into the night and the refuge offered by Ted Grim-

shaw, who was night man at a local mill with the job of attending the boiler. He made Alfie a rough and ready bed of
sacking in the firehole and Alfie enthralled us with his description of this enviable experience. 'It's lovely down
there. All warm. The noise o' the fire roarin' away all the time.
Sends you right off to sleep. And in the mornin' Ted gives me a
big bowl o' water, all hot to wash me in, then he gives me a
mug o' tea fresh-brewed and anythin' that's left over in his
dinner basket for me breakfast.' He added, 'I'd rather have it
there any time than Throstle Nest Mill.'
        'Where's that?'
        'Where we were afore we came here. The night watchman
there used to let me sleep on the bales o' cotton when me dad
was at me. Nice old man, he was, and I wasn't frightened of the
quiet and the dark when I knew he was around with his dog
and I could hear him practising.'
        'Practising what?'
        'Tin whistle. Practising, he said, for when they gave him
the sack and then he could go around all the streets playing on
it and earn pennies. But you give me Ted Grimshaw's firehole any time. Oh, it's lovely and warm down there.'

                                WALTER GREENWOOD, *There Was A Time*

Mother Goes to Bed

When all was in order, one by one, clean clothes under one's
arm, boots in the right hand, candlestick in the left, a plate
with a slice somehow caught between them, a warm maternal
kiss and a 'Good night, God bless' to speed us on our way, we
gingerly, each at his or her appointed hour, made our way to
bed. I should mention the slice. That was a piece of bread to
stave off hunger first thing in the morning. Years of trial and
error had revealed to the children the right substance to coat
it with – golden syrup. By morning this syrup had saturated
the bread and perhaps even crystallized, and the slice tasted
like ambrosia. The slice was usually set on a plate perched
on the clothes on the child's bedside chair, and of course that
has its story too, for Uncle Herbert, one party week-end,
benevolently coming up to see a night-waking child sat down
rather heavily on that child's bedside chair, and adhered to the
slice.

However, what I am leading up to is that my mother was generally the last to come up the stairs. Father had usually retired to bed in dudgeon before she did, to read by his own candle, because he was always irritated by the fact that she could find some new last thing to do, after the absolutely last thing she had already done – raking the ashes of the kitchen range, setting out the clothes to air, letting out the dog Biff, letting in the cat, opening the window, laying the table for morning, boiling the milk in summer lest it went sour and such-like things which only a female imagination could find to worry about at round eleven o'clock or so at night.

Well, then came the business of mother getting to bed. It was a matter of principle to do the thing in one journey. In my mother's view it not only saved time, but it would have been somehow a sign of moral decadence to do the thing in several trips. The back door had to be locked – awake, I often heard the grating slam. The scullery door closed 'to keep in the heat'. Then everything that mother had to gather up from the kitchen table for the morning had to be got hold of. Already laid out would be – *item*, candle, *item*, any clothes to be taken up, *item*, the paper to be finished in bed if she wasn't too tired, *item* the milk can to be set on the front doorstep, *item*, the alarm clock from the kitchen mantelpiece, already set for six-thirty, to be carried up to the table beside mum's bed to rouse the household in the morning. Loaded with all these things, mother had to mount the two steps which led from the kitchen to the passage-way: close the door to keep the heat in – whang, she did that with her bottom. Then she went along the passage, set down the candle and everything else on the door mat, opened the front door, sniffed the air to see what kind of morning it would be in about eight hours' time, put down the milk can (tonkly-clang), slammed the front door (whoof), turned the key (clicketty-click), ran home the bolt (ggrrat-tang!), and picked up all her things carefully, candle still alight (a serious problem in strategy arose when the wind blew the candle out, for my mother was also afraid of the dark) made her way upstairs to the front bedroom, where her impatient husband, anxious probably to sleep, tetched and pshawed with rage.

LESLIE PAUL, *The Boy down Kitchener Street*

MYSTERY

The Listeners

'Is there anybody there?' said the Traveller,
  Knocking on the moonlit door;
And his horse in the silence champ'd the grasses
  Of the forest's ferny floor:
And a bird flew up out of the turret,
  Above the Traveller's head:
And he smote upon the door again a second time;
  'Is there anybody there?' he said.
But no one descended to the Traveller;
  No head from the leaf-fringed sill
Lean'd over and look'd into his grey eyes,
  Where he stood perplex'd and still.
But only a host of phantom listeners
  That dwelt in the lone house then
Stood listening in the quiet of the moonlight
  To that voice from the world of men:
Stood thronging the faint moonbeams on the dark stair,
  That goes down to the empty hall,
Hearkening in an air stirr'd and shaken
  By the lonely Traveller's call.
And he felt in his heart their strangeness,
  Their stillness answering his cry,
While his horse moved, cropping the dark turf,
  'Neath the starr'd and leafy sky;
For he suddenly smote on the door, even
  Louder, and lifted his head: –
'Tell them I came, and no one answer'd,
  That I kept my word,' he said.
Never the least stir made the listeners,
  Though every word he spake
Fell echoing through the shadowiness of the still house
  From the one man left awake:
Ay, they heard his foot upon the stirrup,
  And the sound of iron on stone,
And how the silence surged softly backward,
  When the plunging hoofs were gone.

WALTER DE LA MARE

Flannan Isle

Though three men dwell on Flannan Isle
To keep the lamp alight,
As we steer'd under the lee, we caught
No glimmer through the night.

A passing ship at dawn had brought
The news: and quickly we set sail
To find out what strange thing might ail
The keepers of the deep-sea light.

The winter day broke blue and bright
With glancing sun and glancing spray
As o'er the swell our boat made way,
As gallant as a gull in flight.

But as we near'd the lonely Isle
And look'd up at the naked height,
And saw the lighthouse towering white
With blinded lantern that all night
Had never shot a spark
Of comfort through the dark,
So ghostly in the cold sunlight
It seemed that we were struck the while
With wonder all too dread for words.
And, as into the tiny creek
We stole, beneath the hanging crag
We saw three queer black ugly birds –
Too big by far in my belief
For cormorant or shag –
Like seamen sitting bolt-upright
Upon a half-tide reef:
But as we near'd they plunged from sight
Without a sound or spirt of white.

And still too mazed to speak,
We landed; and made fast the boat
And climbed the track in single file,
Each wishing he was safe afloat
On any sea, however far,
So be it far from Flannan Isle:

And still we seem'd to climb and climb
As though we'd lost all count of time,
And so must climb for evermore;
Yet, all too soon, we reached the door –
The black sun-blister'd lighthouse-door
That gaped for us ajar.

As on the threshold for a spell
We paused, we seem'd to breathe the smell
Of limewash and of tar,
Familiar as our daily breath,
As though 'twere some strange scent of death;
And so yet wondering side by side,
We stood a moment, still tongue-tied,
And each with black foreboding eyed
The door ere we should fling it wide
To leave the sunlight for the gloom:
Till, plucking courage up, at last
Hard on each other's heels we pass'd
Into the living room.

Yet, as we crowded through the door
We only saw a table, spread
For dinner, meat and cheese and bread,
But all untouch'd; and no one there;
As though when they sat down to eat,
Ere they could even taste,
Alarm had come and they in haste
Had risen and left the bread and meat,
For at the table-head a chair
Lay tumbled on the floor.

We listened, but we only heard
The feeble cheeping of a bird
That starved upon its perch;
And, listening still, without a word
We set about our hopeless search.
We hunted high, we hunted low,
And soon ransacked the empty house;
Then o'er the Island, to and fro
We ranged, to listen and to look
In every cranny, cleft or nook

That might have hid a bird or mouse:
But though we searched from shore to shore
We found no sign in any place,
And soon again stood face to face
Before the gaping door,
And stole into the room once more
As frighten'd children steal.
Ay, though we hunted high and low
And hunted everywhere,
Of the three men's fate we found no trace
Of any kind in any place
But a door ajar and an untouch'd meal
And an overtoppled chair.

And as we listen'd in the gloom
Of that forsaken living-room –
A chill clutch on our breath –
We thought how ill-chance came to all
Who kept the Flannan Light,
And how the rock had been the death
Of many a likely lad –
How six had come to a sudden end
And three had gone stark mad,
And one, whom we'd all known as friend,
Had leapt from the lantern one still night
And fallen dead by the lighthouse wall –
And long we thought
On the three we sought,
And of what might yet befall.

Like curs a glance has brought to heel
We listen'd, flinching there,
And looked and looked on the untouched meal
And the overtoppled chair.

We seemed to stand for an endless while,
Though still no word was said,
Three men alive on Flannan Isle
Who thought on three men dead.

                                        W. W. GIBSON

The Cold Duke

Once upon a time, in a gloomy castle on a lonely hill, where there were thirteen clocks that wouldn't go, there lived a cold, aggressive Duke, and his niece, the Princess Saralinda. She was warm in every wind and weather, but he was always cold. His hands were as cold as his smile and almost as cold as his heart. He wore gloves when he was asleep, and he wore gloves when he was awake, which made it difficult for him to pick up pins or coins or the kernels of nuts, or to tear the wings from nightingales. He was six feet four, and forty-six, and even colder than he thought he was. One eye wore a velvet patch; the other glittered through a monocle, which made half his body seem closer to you than the other half. He had lost one eye when he was twelve, for he was fond of peering into nests and lairs in search of birds and animals to maul. One afternoon, a mother shrike had mauled him first. His nights were spent in evil dreams, and his days were given to wicked schemes.

Wickedly scheming, he would limp and cackle through the cold corridors of the castle, planning new impossible feats for the suitors of Saralinda to perform. He did not wish to give her hand in marriage, since her hand was the only warm hand in the castle. Even the hands of his watch and the hands of all the thirteen clocks were frozen. They had all been frozen at the same time, on a snowy night, seven years before, and after that it was always ten minutes to five in the castle. Travellers and mariners would look up at the gloomy castle on the lonely hill and say, 'Time lies frozen there. It's always Then. It's never Now.'

JAMES THURBER, *The 13 Clocks*

The Taking of the Golden Fleece

'Tomorrow you shall have the Golden Fleece,' promised Aeëtes: but before then he plotted to burn the *Argo* and murder the Argonauts.

Medea again came to Jason, and warned him, and in the night she led him and Orpheus to the magic garden where the Golden Fleece hung on the Tree at the World's End, guarded by a dragon – just as the Apples of the Hesperides hung in their garden at the World's opposite end.

It was a dim, mysterious place, high-walled and pillared with the dark boles of mighty trees. Through the dappling moonlight Medea the Witch-Maiden led the way, until they came to the centre where the Golden Fleece shone in the darkness as it hung from a tree round which coiled a dragon larger and more terrible than any in the world.

'Play and sing!' whispered Medea to Orpheus, and she began to murmur a spell while he touched gently on the strings of his lyre and sang in a sweet low voice his Hymn to Sleep:

> 'Sleep, king of gods and men,
>   Master of all;
> Come to mine eyes again,
>   Come as I call!
> Sleep, who may loose and bind
>   Each as his thrall,
> Come to the weary mind,
>   Come at my call!
> Tamer of toil and woes,
>   Healer of all;
> Sleep, whence our solace flows,
>   Come as I call!
> Brother of all mankind,
>   Softly you fall
> Leaving the world behind:
>   Come at my call!
> Sleep, lord of all things made,
>   Sleep over all
> Let your warm wings be laid,
>   Come as I call!'

As Orpheus sang it seemed that the very garden slept: the wind grew still; the flowers drooped their heads, and not a leaf stirred. The great gleaming dragon slid slowly from the tree, coil within coil, and, resting its terrible head on a bank of sleeping red poppies, slept for the first and last time in its life.

Only by the charms of Medea did Jason himself remain awake, and when he saw that the dragon slept, he drew near and looked up at the shining Fleece.

Then Medea sprinkled the dragon with her magic brew, and whispered to Jason:

'Climb! Climb swiftly up the coils of its back and take down the Fleece, for my charms will not hold it long!'

So Jason, not without dread, mounted that terrible ladder into the great ilex-tree[1] and unhooked the Golden Fleece which had hung there ever since Phrixus stripped it from the magic Ram; and by its light he found his way through the garden.

For Medea, by her charms, called for Hecate, the Immortal Queen of the Witches, and by her help the moon was darkened, and night closed over Colchis like a black cloak.

ROGER LANCELYN GREEN, *Tales of the Greek Heroes*

SCHOOLS AND SCHOOLTEACHERS

'My parents kept me from children who were rough'

My parents kept me from children who were rough
Who threw words like stones and who wore torn clothes.
Their thighs showed through rags. They ran in the street
And climbed cliffs and stripped by the country streams.

I feared more than tigers their muscles like iron
Their jerking hands and their knees tight on my arms.
I feared the salt coarse pointing of those boys
Who copied my lisp behind me on the road.

They were lithe, they sprang out behind hedges
Like dogs to bark at my world. They threw mud
While I looked the other way, pretending to smile.
I longed to forgive them, but they never smiled.

STEPHEN SPENDER

The Lesson

'Your father's gone,' my bald headmaster said.
His shiny dome and brown tobacco jar

[1] Holm-oak, genus including common holly.

Splintered at once in tears. It wasn't grief.
I cried for knowledge which was bitterer
Than any grief. For there and then I knew
That grief has uses – that a father dead
Could bind the bully's fist a week or two;
And then I cried for shame, then for relief.

I was a month past ten when I learnt this:
I still remember how the noise was stilled
In school-assembly when my grief came in.
Some goldfish in a bowl quietly sculled
Around their shining prison on its shelf.
They were indifferent. All the other eyes
Were turned towards me. Somewhere in myself
Pride, like a goldfish, flashed a sudden fin.

EDWARD LUCIE-SMITH

The First Day at School

He was a little boy named Jim, the first and only child of Dr
Louis Davy, 717 Mattei Building, and it was his first day at
school. His father was French, a small heavy-set man of
forty whose boyhood had been full of poverty and unhappiness
and ambition. His mother was dead: she died when Jim was
born, and the only woman he knew intimately was Amy, the
Swedish housekeeper.

It was Amy who dressed him in his Sunday clothes and
took him to school. Jim liked Amy, but he didn't like her for
taking him to school. He told her so. All the way to school, he
told her so.

I don't like you, he said.
I don't like you any more.
I like *you*, the housekeeper said.
Then why are you taking me to school? he said.
He had taken walks with Amy before, once all the way to the
Court House Park for the Sunday afternoon band concert, but
this walk to school was different.
What for? he said.
Everybody must go to school, the housekeeper said.
Did you go to school? he said.
No, said Amy.

Then why do I have to go? he said.

You will like it, said the housekeeper.

He walked on with her in silence, holding her hand. I don't like you, he said. I don't like you any more.

I like you, said Amy.

Then why are you taking me to school? he said again. Why?

The housekeeper knew how frightened a little boy could be about going to school.

You will like it, she said. I think you will sing songs and play games.

I don't want to, he said.

I will come and get you every afternoon, she said.

I don't like you, he told her again.

She felt very unhappy about the little boy going to school, but she knew that he would have to go.

The school building was very ugly to her and to the boy. She didn't like the way it made her feel, and going up the steps with him she wished he didn't have to go to school. The halls and rooms scared her, and him, and the smell of the place too. And he didn't like Mr Barber, the principal.

Amy despised Mr Barber.

What is the name of your son? Mr Barber said.

This is Dr Louis Davy's son, said Amy. His name is Jim. I am Dr Davy's housekeeper.

James? said Mr Barber.

Not James, said Amy, just Jim.

All right, said Mr Barber. Any middle name?

No, said Amy. He is too small for a middle name. Just Jim Davy.

All right, said Mr Barber. We'll try him out in the first grade. If he doesn't get along all right we'll try him out in kindergarten.

Dr Davy said to start him in the first grade, said Amy. Not kindergarten.

All right, said Mr Barber.

The housekeeper knew how frightened the little boy was, sitting on the chair, and she tried to let him know how much she loved him and how sorry she was about everything. She wanted to say something fine to him about everything, but she couldn't say anything, and she was very proud of the nice way he got down from the chair and stood beside Mr Barber, waiting to go with him to a classroom.

On the way home she was so proud of him she began to cry.

Miss Binney, the teacher of the first grade, was an old lady who was all dried out. The room was full of little boys and girls. School smelled strange and sad. He sat at a desk and listened carefully.

He heard some of the names: Charles, Ernest, Alvin, Norman, Betty, Hannah, Juliet, Viola, Polly.

He listened carefully and heard Miss Binney say, Hannah Winter, what *are* you chewing? And he saw Hannah Winter blush. He liked Hannah Winter right from the beginning.

Gum, said Hannah.

Put it in the waste-basket, said Miss Binney.

He saw the little girl walk to the front of the class, take the gum from her mouth, and drop it into the waste-basket.

And he heard Miss Binney say, Ernest Gaskin, what are *you* chewing?

Gum, said Ernest.

And he liked Ernest Gaskin too.

They met in the schoolyard, and Ernest taught him a few jokes.

Amy was in the hall when school ended. She was sullen and angry at everybody until she saw the little boy. She was amazed that he wasn't changed, that he wasn't hurt, or perhaps utterly unalive, murdered. The school and everything about it frightened her very much. She took his hand and walked out of the building with him, feeling angry and proud.

Jim said, What comes after twenty-nine?

Thirty, said Amy.

Your face is dirty, he said.

His father was very quiet at the supper table.

What comes after twenty-nine? the boy said.

Thirty, said his father.

Your face is dirty, he asked.

In the morning he asked his father for a nickel.

What do you want a nickel for? his father said.

Gum, he said.

His father gave him a nickel and on the way to school he stopped at Mrs Riley's store and bought a package of Spearmint.

Do you want a piece? he asked Amy.

Do you want to give me a piece? the housekeeper said.

Jim thought about it a moment, and then he said, Yes.

Do you like me? said the housekeeper.

I like you, said Jim. Do you like me?

Yes, said the housekeeper.

Do you like school?

Jim didn't know for sure, but he knew he liked the part about the gum. And Hannah Winter. And Ernest Gaskin.

I don't know, he said.

Do you sing? asked the housekeeper.

No, we don't sing, he said.

Do you play games? she said.

Not in school, he said. In the yard we do.

He liked the part about the gum very much.

Miss Binney said, Jim Davy, what are you *chewing?*

Ha, ha, ha, he thought.

Gum, he said.

He walked to the waste-paper basket and back to his seat, and Hannah Winter saw him, and Ernest Gaskin too. That was the best part of school.

It began to grow too.

Ernest Gaskin, he shouted in the schoolyard, *what* are you *chewing?*

Raw elephant meat, said Ernest Gaskin. Jim Davy, what are *you* chewing?

Jim tried to think of something very funny to be chewing, but he couldn't.

Gum, he said, and Ernest Gaskin laughed louder than Jim laughed when Ernest Gaskin said raw elephant meat.

It was funny no matter what you said.

Going back to the classroom Jim saw Hannah Winter in the hall.

Hannah Winter, he said, *what in the world* are you *chewing?*

The little girl was startled. She wanted to say something nice that would honestly show how nice she felt about having Jim say her name, and ask her the funny question, making fun of school, but she couldn't think of anything that nice to say because they were almost in the room, and there wasn't time enough.

Tutti-frutti, she said with desperate haste.

Amy Larson, he said, *what, are, you, chewing?*

He told his father all about it at the supper table.

He said, Once there was a hill. On the hill there was a mill.
Under the mill there was a walk. Under the walk there was a
key. What is it?
I don't know, said his father. What is it?
Milwaukee, said the boy.
The housekeeper was delighted.
Mill. Walk. Key, Jim said.
Tutti-frutti.
What's that? said his father.
Gum, he said. The kind Hannah Winter chews.
Who's Hannah Winter? said his father.
She's in my room, he said.
Oh, said his father.
After supper he sat on the floor with the small red and blue
and yellow top that hummed while it spinned. It was all right,
he guessed. It was still very sad, but the gum part of it was very
funny and the Hannah Winter part very nice. Raw elephant
meat, he thought with great inward delight.
Raw elephant meat, he said aloud to his father who was
reading the evening paper. His father folded the paper and sat
on the floor beside him.
The housekeeper saw them together on the floor and for
some reason tears came to her eyes.

WILLIAM SAROYAN, *Little Children*

The Fun they had

Margie even wrote about it that night in her diary. On the
page headed 17 May, 2155, she wrote, 'Today Tommy found
a real book!'
It was a very old book. Margie's grandfather once said that
when he was a little boy *his* grandfather told him that there
was a time when all stories were printed on paper.
They turned the pages, which were yellow and crinkly, and
it was awfully funny to read words that stood still instead of
moving the way they were supposed to – on a screen, you
know. And then, when they turned back to the page before,
it had the same words on it that it had had when they read it
the first time.
'Gee,' said Tommy, 'what a waste. When you're through
with the book, you just throw it away, I guess. Our television

screen must have had a million books on it and it's good for
plenty more. I wouldn't throw *it* away.'

'Same with mine,' said Margie. She was eleven and hadn't
seen as many telebooks as Tommy had. He was thirteen.

She said, 'Where did you find it?'

'In my house.' He pointed without looking, because he was
busy reading. 'In the attic.'

'What's it about?'

'School.'

Margie was scornful. 'School? What's there to write about
school? I hate school.' Margie always hated school, but now
she hated it more than ever. The mechanical teacher had been
giving her test after test in geography and she had been doing
worse and worse until her mother had shaken her head sorrow-
fully and sent for the County Inspector.

He was a round little man with a red face and a whole box of
tools with dials and wires. He smiled at her and gave her an
apple, then took the teacher apart. Margie had hoped he
wouldn't know how to put it together again, but he knew how
all right and after an hour or so, there it was again, large and
black and ugly with a big screen on which all the lessons were
shown and the questions were asked. That wasn't so bad. The
part she hated most was the slot where she had to put homework and test papers. She always had to write them out in a
punch code they made her learn when she was six years old,
and the mechanical teacher calculated the mark in no time.

The Inspector had smiled after he was finished and patted
her head. He said to her mother, 'It's not the little girl's fault,
Mrs Jones. I think the geography sector was geared a little too
quick. Those things happen sometimes. I've slowed it up to
an average ten-year level. Actually, the overall pattern of her
progress is quite satisfactory.' And he patted Margie's head
again.

Margie was disappointed. She had been hoping they would
take the teacher away altogether. They had once taken
Tommy's teacher away for nearly a month because the history
sector had blanked out completely.

So she said to Tommy, 'Why would anyone write about
school?'

Tommy looked at her with very superior eyes. 'Because it's
not our kind of school, stupid. This is the old kind of school
that they had hundreds and hundreds of years ago.' He added

loftily, pronouncing the word carefully, *'Centuries* ago.'

Margie was hurt. 'Well, I don't know what kind of school they had all that time ago.' She read the book over his shoulder for a while, then said, 'Anyway, they had a teacher.'

'Sure they had a teacher, but it wasn't a *regular* teacher. It was a man.'

'A man? How could a man be a teacher?'

'Well, he just told the boys and girls things and gave them homework and asked them questions.'

'A man isn't smart enough.'

'Sure he is. My father knows as much as my teacher.'

'He can't. A man can't know as much as a teacher.'

'He knows almost as much, I betcha.'

Margie wasn't prepared to dispute that. She said, 'I wouldn't want a strange man in my house to teach me.'

Tommy screamed with laughter. 'You don't know much, Margie. The teachers didn't live in the house. They had a special building and all the kids went there.'

'And all the kids learned the same thing?'

'Sure, if they were the same age.'

'But my mother says a teacher has to be adjusted to fit the mind of each boy and girl it teaches and that each kid has to be taught differently.'

'Just the same they didn't do it that way then. If you don't like it, you don't have to read the book.'

'I didn't say I didn't like it,' Margie said quickly. She wanted to read about those funny schools.

They weren't even half finished when Margie's mother called, 'Margie! School!'

Margie looked up. 'Not yet, mamma.'

'Now,' said Mrs. Jones. 'And it's probably time for Tommy, too.'

Margie said to Tommy, 'Can I read the book some more with you after school?'

'Maybe,' he said, nonchalantly. He walked away whistling, the dusty old book tucked beneath his arm.

Margie went into the schoolroom. It was right next to her bedroom, and the mechanical teacher was on and waiting for her. It was always on at the same time every day except Saturday and Sunday, because her mother said little girls learned better if they learned at regular hours.

The screen was lit up, and it said: 'Today's arithmetic

lesson is on the addition of proper fractions. Please insert yesterday's homework in the proper slot.'

Margie did so with a sigh. She was thinking about the old schools they had when her grandfather's grandfather was a little boy. All the kids from the whole neighbourhood came, laughing and shouting in the school-yard, sitting together in the schoolroom, going home together at the end of the day. They learned the same things so they could help one another on the homework and talk about it.

And the teachers were people . . .

The mechanical teacher was flashing on the screen: 'When we add the fractions $\frac{1}{2}$ and $\frac{1}{4}$ –'

Margie was thinking about how the kids must have loved it in the old days. She was thinking about the fun they had.

ISAAC ASIMOV

PATTERN POEMS

Sailing Homeward

Cliffs that rise a thousand feet
Without a break,
Lake that stretches a hundred miles
Without a wave,
Sands that are white through all the year
Without a stain,
Pine-tree woods, winter and summer
Ever-green,
Streams that for ever flow and flow
Without a pause,
Trees that for twenty thousand years
Your vows have kept,
You have suddenly healed the pain of a traveller's heart,
And moved his brush to write a new song.

CHAN FANG-SHENG (4th century A.D.), translated ARTHUR WALEY

Green, green

Green, green,
The grass by the river-bank.
Thick, thick,
The willow trees in the garden.
Sad, sad,
The lady in the tower.
White, white,
Sitting at the casement window.
Fair, fair,
Her red-powdered face.
Small, small,
She puts out her pale hand.
Once she was a dancing-house girl,
Now she is a wandering man's wife.
The wandering man went, but did not return.
It is hard alone to keep an empty bed.

AUTHOR UNKNOWN (about 1st century B.C. or 1st century A.D.) translated
ARTHUR WALEY

Here

Here clay
cool coal clings
to glass, creates
clinks, silica glitters,
children of stars.
Here cool
dew falls
in the evening
black
birds blink
on the tree
stump ravished
with fire
ruined with its
gold.

EDWARD BRAITHWAITE

Here's a Little Mouse

here's a little mouse) and
what does he think about, i
wonder as over this
floor (quietly with

bright eyes) drifts (nobody
can tell because
Nobody knows, or why
jerks Here &, here,
gr(oo)ving the room's Silence) this like
a littlest
poem a
(with wee ears and see?

tail frisks)
                    (gonE)
'mouse',
              We are not the same you and

i, since here's a little he
or is
it It
? (or something we saw in the mirror)?

therefore we'll kiss; for maybe
what was Disappeared
into ourselves
who (look).   , startled

                                    e. e. cummings

Hunger

I come among the peoples like a shadow.
I sit down by each man's side.

None sees me, but they look on one another,
And know that I am there.

My silence is like the silence of the tide
That buries the playground of children;

Like the deepening of frost in the slow night,
When the birds are dead in the morning.

Armies trample, invade, destroy,
With guns roaring from earth and air.

I am more terrible than armies,
I am more feared than the cannon.

Kings and chancellors give commands;
I give no command to any;

But I am listened to more than kings
And more than passionate orators.

I unswear words, and undo deeds.
Naked things know me.

I am first and last to be felt of the living.
I am Hunger.

LAWRENCE BINYON

A CHAPTER

The Golden Seal

The little boy had no difficulty in fording the river; the water was barely up to his ankles. Then, with many a backward glance to be sure he was keeping the *barabara*[1] in sight, he started up the bank. In one hand were his father's binoculars, in the other a rhododendron branch with which he flicked the melting medusas[2] out of his path. In twenty minutes he was on top of the highest sand-dune.

The view was magnificent. Behind him the river snaking the slopes of Shishaldin[3]; to his left the estuary, with the *barabara* a pinpoint on its farther shore (it was still in sight if he got it in the viewfinder of the binoculars, so he hadn't *really* broken his promise); and in front of him the vast expanse of sea kelp, unbroken and brown as a salmon berry. He focused the glasses on it.

He couldn't make out at first what was wrong; couldn't understand why, in the viewfinder of the binoculars, the image of the kelp kept on blurring and slipping out of focus. It seemed to be moving. It was several minutes before he

[1] A turf hut, built partly or wholly underground and found in Alaska or northern Siberia.
[2] Jelly-fish.
[3] Sheshaldin Volcano on Unimak Island in South Western Alaska.

realized it really *was* moving, was undulating up and down in wide-spaced rhythmic swells. Eric was fascinated. He lay face down on the stones, legs wide apart, glasses riveted on the moving mosaic of kelp. All else was forgotten; golden seals, parents, storm; he was rapt in his discovery, lost to the world. He didn't see the great copper-coloured cloud flooding out against the wind from behind the spire of Shishaldin, he didn't see the stir of the sedge grass in the hot sirocco [1] wind. Only when the sea kelp split and the spume came scudding inland and the waves began to pound the shore did he realize something was wrong.

He jumped up. He spun round. He saw the great cloud swallowing the sky. In terror he stood irresolute, like a seabird poised for flight, a wind-torn papier-mâché silhouette dwarfed by the immensity of sea and cloud. Then he began to run.

Nine boys out of ten (nine hundred and ninety-nine town-bred boys out of a thousand) would have run for home, for the reassuring arms of their parents. But Eric ran for the sod hut, for the nearest of the dozen or so shelters built along the crest of the bank. That was the lesson his father had always drummed into him: 'If you're out in a storm take shelter at once; never get caught in the open.' The sod hut was nearer than the *barabara* and so he ran for the sod hut.

He ran for his life, his feet sinking and slipping on the loose-packed stones, while about him the sky grew darker, the wind stronger and the bank began to tremble to the pound of steepening waves. At last his goal was in sight – the squat mound of turves sunk igloo-like into the ground. He was within a hundred yards of it when the light went suddenly out of the sky. A gust of wind knocked him off his feet. He didn't get up. He shook his head and crawled on. Beneath him the stones began to shift, and loose sand to stream in tattered pennants off the crests of the sand-dunes. He kept his face close to the gravel and crawled on. It seemed a very long way to the shelter. After a while he began to doubt if he'd have the strength to reach it; but at last his fingers were clawing at the circle of sods.

---

[1] Not accurately used. The term properly refers to an oppressive hot south or south-east wind, humid or dry, blowing from the North African coast across the area of southern Italy.

He collapsed face down on the threshold, gasping for breath. And the first thing he noticed was the smell. For a second he drew back, uncertain. Then the gravel beat stinging against his legs, and he squirmed quickly in.

The sod hut was small and dark; it had no window or chimney; its door was simply a couple of movable turves which Eric, from the inside, now hauled-to to keep out the wind. As the turves were pulled in the moan of the storm faded, the last glimmer of light was snuffed out, and the smell – strong and foetid – rose pungently out of the dark. On the far side of the sod hut something moved.

The little boy peered into the darkness, suddenly afraid.

Twin orbs of fire swayed up from the floor: twin balls of red aglow like oriflammes[1] in the dark. And Eric shrank back, appalled. Something was in the sod hut: some wild and terrible animal – perhaps a great Kodiak bear with foot-long claws that could rip the guts from a caribou in a single slash. He spun round. He tore at the door turves. Then he remembered the storm.

He stood very still, teeth clenched, eyes screwed tight. Waiting. But the wild and terrible animal didn't spring at him. Everything was motionless and very quiet – everything except his heart which was pounding in frightened leaps between mouth and stomach, and after a while even the pound of his heart sank to a muffled uncertain throb. Hesitantly he unscrewed his eyes, ready to snap them shut the moment the animal moved. But the orbs of red were motionless. The creature – whatever it was – kept to the farther side of the hut.

He peered into the blackness. At first he could see only the red of the eyes, but gradually as he became accustomed to the dark he could make out more: a shadowy mass, coiled and menacing, stretching almost a third of the way round the wall. The animal was large; but – to his unspeakable relief – it wasn't thickset and solid enough to be a bear. He began to breathe more easily.

After a while he became conscious of a faint persistent sound: a sound so low that it had been drowned up to now by the thud of his heart and the background moan of the storm. It was a sucky, slobbery sound: a sound he had heard before –

---

[1] Little streamers or banners of red silk.

years and years ago when he was very small; it wasn't a sound
to be frightened of; he knew that; its associations were
pleasant. His fear ebbed a little. Perhaps the creature was
friendly; perhaps it would let him stay; perhaps the hut was a
refuge they could both, in time of emergency, share.

His mind seized on to the idea, thankfully. He remembered
a picture in one of his story-books: a picture of a little boy (no
older than he was) and all sorts of different animals lying together on a flood-ringed island; and he remembered his father
reading the caption, 'Then the wolf shall dwell with the lamb,
and the leopard shall lie down with the kid, and the calf and
the young lion and the fatling together,' and he remembered
his father explaining that in times of great danger – fire or
flood, tempest or drought – all living things reverted to their
natural (sinless) state and lived peacefully together until the
danger was passed. This, he told himself, must be such a time.

He stared at the glowing eyes. And quite suddenly his fear
was submerged in a great flood of curiosity. What *was* this
strange red-eyed creature? It was too big for a fox or a hare,
and not the right shape for a bear or a caribou. If only he could
see it!

He remembered then that somewhere in every sod hut his
father had cached matches and candles.

An older boy would have hesitated now. An older boy would
have had second thoughts and a legacy of fear. But to Eric
things were uncomplicated. He *had* been frightened, but that
was in the past: *now* he was curious. For a little boy of seven it
was as simple as that.

He felt round the wall until his hand struck a metal box. He
prized off the lid. He found and lit one of the candles. A
flickering light leapt round the hut. And the little boy's
breath stuck in his throat and he could only stare and stare.
For never in all his life had he seen anything so beautiful.

She lay curled up against the wall: a sinuous seven-foot
golden seal, her fur like a field of sun-drenched corn; and
clinging to her teats two soft-furred pups, their eyes still
closed.

'Ooooh!' he whispered.

Holding the candle high, his fear quite lost in wonder, he
walked towards her.

'Ooooh!' he whispered. 'You're beautiful. An' your babies.'

One of the pups, frightened by his voice, fell away from its

mother and went snuffling round the floor. He bent down to pick it up.

The golden seal drew in her head. Her lips writhed back. Her eyes turned suddenly dark.

'It's all right,' the little boy said softly, 'you needn't be scared. I know what to do.'

And very gently he picked up the pup and clamped it back on its teat.

A hint of hesitation or fear and she would have killed him. But his assurance took her aback; her head swayed this way and that like a cobra's, but she didn't strike.

He looked at her brightly. 'I bet you're hungry. Let's find something to eat.'

And he turned his back on her and started to forage inside the tin.

In it he found all manner of intriguing things: bandages, blocks of solid fuel and food – bars of chocolate and cuts of *beleek*-smoked salmon. He didn't know how to use the fuel, but the food he sorted into two piles.

'The chocolate's for me,' he told the golden seal. 'The salmon's for you.'

She looked at him balefully. When he pushed the food towards her she didn't touch it. She watched his every move.

He stood the candle on the base of the upturned tin, and its flaring light threw shadows a-dance on the curve of the walls. He went to the door and eased out one of the turves. But for a second only. For the storm was raging now with sustained malevolence, and the bank was a place of death, a battleground of wind and spume and ripped-up gravel and sand.

But inside the sod hut it was sheltered and almost cosy. The little boy and the golden seal lay either side of the circle of candlelight and stared at each other.

And the hours passed.

Every now and then Eric pulled aside one of the turves to see if the storm was easing off, but its violence remained unabated, hour after hour. Every now and then he renewed the candles – they burnt fast in the eddying draughts. And in between times he ate chocolate, bar after bar of it. And every time he ate a bar of chocolate he laid out a salmon cut for the golden seal. At first she wouldn't look at it. But eventually, about the time that behind the storm clouds the sun was dipping under the ice-blink, she reached out her neck and sniffed at and tasted the nearest cut. She liked it. The little boy gave her more. And it was not very long before she was letting him put the fish into her mouth.

Come sundown the temperature dropped sharply. The wind backed and the rain hardened to snow. Eric began to shiver. He unearthed the blankets, cached alongside the tin of provisions. There were two of them. He wrapped himself in one and the other he draped carefully over the gold-furred seal.

And the hours passed, each slower and colder than the one before.

They lay either side of the hut. Between them the guttering candle, outside the moan of the wind and the drifting up of the snow, and above the storm clouds the anaemic stars creeping conspirator-like into a frightened sky. The night grew darker. The snow drifted higher. The candle burnt lower. Its wick drooped into the melted wax. The flame was snuffed out. A pencil of smoke coiled up to the roof sods. And the little boy slept.

He woke in the small cold hours of the morning, stiff, uncomfortable and trembling. The hut smelt of smoke, candlegrease, fish and excrement, and the gravel was rimmed with frost. He was lost and cold and oh so miserably alone. He tried to wrap himself more warmly into the blanket; but the blanket was all sides and ends – not big enough to keep out of the cold.

For a while he rocked to and fro, trying to comfort himself. Then he began to cry. He cried noiselessly, the tears welling out in a steady flood, salting his cheeks, trickling round the corners of his mouth and dropping forlornly into a fold in the blanket. It was the loneliness that frightened him most.

On the far side of the hut the golden seal stirred. Her head swayed up; her eyes glowed warm and red.

Eric stopped crying. He stared at the eyes, mesmerized. Then unthinkingly, half-asleep, half-awake, his blanket dragging behind him, he crawled across to her. Awkwardly in the dark he snuggled against her. She was soft and warm and comforting. And she didn't snarl at him.

Soon his shivering, like his tears, died away. And it was not very long before he fell asleep, his face buried deep in the fine-spun gold of her fur.

During the night he slipped lower, and by dawn he was wedged against the warmth of her teats and her pups were snuffling hungrily. She nuzzled him aside. He fell to the ground; the cold and hardness of the stones jerked him awake, and he sat up stretching and yawning.

The air in the sod hut was heavy and stale, and he went to the doorway and tried to ease out the turves. They were stuck. He kicked them impatiently, and they cracked open and ice, wind and snow came swirling into the hut.

It was an unfamiliar world he peered out on. The sky hung low, a livid sheet wiped clear of colouring or cloud, and across it streamed the wind, a wind robbed now of its former malevolence but still strong enough to bowl a man off his feet and to drive in front of it a continuous veil of snow. The storm was dying, but it was not yet dead.

Thoughtfully Eric pulled back the turves; thoughtfully he looked at the seal. And he was troubled. For it came to him that now the weather was improving his father would soon be starting to search for him; and didn't his father often go hunting golden seals – with a gun?

The idea appalled him. It was unthinkable that 'she with the yellow hair' should be hurt. She was his friend. He sat down, head in hands, thinking. And after a while and with delightful clarity the answer came to him. He must make certain he found his father before his father found the golden seal; and he must make him promise never to hurt her.

Having hit on his plan he was eager to be off – at the back of
his mind was a nagging fear that his father might appear unexpectedly and shoot the seal before he had a chance to explain. He stuffed the last of the chocolate into his pocket; he
fed the last of the fish to the golden seal, and as soon as he
could stand against the ever-lessening tear of the wind he set
off for the *barabara*.

In the doorway of the hut he paused and looked back. His
eyes met the golden seal's.

'Don't you worry,' he said, 'I'll see nobody shoots you.'

JAMES VANCE MARSHALL, A River Ran out of Eden

SHORT STORY

The Sorrel Colt

Tired of playing 'Tiger', a game of his own invention which
consisted of chasing through the tree-tops after his brother
Leo, who defended himself bravely, using the green figs as
ammunition, Mario went out to the back gate of the villa; and
there, in the noonday sun, he leaned against one of the old
pillars and gazed at the street, waiting patiently for Leo, still
perched on the topmost branch of a fig tree and eager to continue the fight, to grow weary of shouting 'Nitwit!' and 'Jackass!' at him – when an unexpected sight filled him with
pleasant surprise.

Turning the corner of the villa, a man riding a pot-bellied
mare, followed by a tiny little colt, had just appeared on the
street, and was slowly approaching.

'Say!'

And Mario, with his eyes wide open and his face beaming,
went to the edge of the path to get a better view of the procession.

'A colt!' . . . One would have to know how much it meant,
then, to Mario, to get a colt of his own, that is, a horse in pro-
portion to his size! . . .

This was his 'fad', his passion, his everlasting dream. But,
unfortunately – and this he knew from experience – his
parents wanted no animals at the villa because they would eat

up the plants and strip the bark off the tree-trunks.

Over at 'The Ranch', anything their hearts desired: namely, a docile little pony, old and big-headed. But here, at the villa, no 'beasts' at all!

For this reason, Mario was about to resign himself, as on other occasions, to watch indifferently the little marvel's passing, when an extraordinary thing happened.

Just as he came face to face with him, without slackening his trot and almost without turning his face, the man riding the mare, a big robust young fellow with a sullen face and a red beret, let loose to Mario with this wonderful proposal.

'Hey, kid! . . . If you want this colt, I'll give him to you. I'm taking him out in the fields to kill him!'

When Mario heard this, he felt the ground quake under his feet, his eyes cloud over, and the blood rush to his head; but oh! he knew the rules of the house so thoroughly that he didn't hesitate a second and, red as a tomato, he refused, ashamed:

'No . . . Thank you . . . no!'

The brawny young man shrugged his shoulders slightly and, without another word, went his way through the sunlight that flooded the street, while following the weary gait of his mare, came that marvelous sorrel colt, who trotted proudly over the clods of dried mud and who, with his fluffy, yellowish tail, tried to brush off the flies just like a grown-up horse.

'Mamma! . . .'

And dashing headlong like a colt and without time to say anything to his brother, who, ignorant of everything and still at the top of his fig-tree, took advantage of his swift flight to pelt him with a few figs, Mario appeared under the arbour, stumbling over everything in his path:

'Oh Mamma! Oh Mamma!'

His mother, who was sewing in her arm-chair in the shade of the young vines, rose from her chair with a start:

'Good Heavens, son, what's the matter?'

'Nothing, mamma, nothing . . . just a man!'

'What, son, what?'

'Just a man was driving a beautiful little colt, and he wanted to give it to me! . . .'

'Mercy, what a fright you gave me!' Then his mother smiled; but he, in his excitement, went on without hearing her.

'A beautiful little colt, mamma, a tiny little sorrel colt, this big . . . and the man was going to kill him, mamma!'

And now something else stupendous happened, for contrary to all expectations and logic, Mario heard his mother say, with genuine concern:

'Really? . . . Well! . . . Why didn't you accept it, silly? Specially now that we're going to "The Ranch".'

In the face of so unusual, so unjustified, and so surprising a remark, his jaw dropped a foot, but he was so 'colt crazy' that he didn't stop to ask questions and with an 'I'll call him, then,' as vibrant and shrill as a neigh, he started running towards the gate.

'Careful, son!' cried his mother.

Careful nothing! . . . Mario ran so fast that his brother didn't manage to throw a single fig at him as he passed.

When he went out on to the street, the sun's glare dazzled him. Not a single colt or mare or man anywhere . . . But soon his anxious eyes caught a glimpse of the red beret, off there in the distance, bobbing along in the rhythm of a trot in a cloud of dust.

And in vain the ridges of dry mud made him stumble and fall several times, in vain he felt choked up with emotion, in vain the laundress's hateful little curs came out to greet him – nothing nor anyone could stop Mario from running.

Inside of two blocks he was within earshot of the supreme arbiter of his happiness, who was moseying along dejectedly at a trot on a humble, pot-bellied mare.

'Hey! Hey! Mister, mister! . . .'

When the brawny young man heard him, he reined in his mount and waited for Mario, frowning hard.

'What do you want, huh?'

'The colt! . . . I want the colt!' Mario panted breathlessly and he stretched out his arms towards the animal, as if they were to receive it, like a package in a store.

The man made a doubtful, wry face.

'All right,' he said. 'Take hold of him.' And at once he added, looking down at his hands:

'Did you bring something to do it with?'

Mario blushed again.

'No . . . I didn't . . .'

He looked around, embarrassed, as though he expected to find a halter hidden somewhere in the grass . . .

The man dismounted and went to unhook a piece of wire that happened to be hanging from the thorny cina-cina[1] fence, while the boy watched him, filled with emotion.

II

Only Mario knew what it meant to him – that little sorrel colt who destroyed plants, who bit and kicked, who refused to budge when he didn't want to; who once tore out a lock of Mario's hair with one bite, probably thinking it was grass, but who ate sugar from his hand and neighed as soon as he saw him in the distance! . . .

He was his love, his worry, his guiding star, his spiritual light. So much so, that his parents became accustomed to using the colt as a means of taming the little boy, and keeping him in line.

If you don't study, you can't go out on the colt this afternoon . . . If you misbehave, we'll take away the colt . . . If you do this or don't do that . . .'

Always the colt loomed up against Mario's rebellions like the elaborate standard of some invincible legion in the thick of battle.

The threat had such power over him that in no time he would sheathe his arrogance just as any fighter sheathes his knife at the arrival of the sheriff. For that sorrel colt was such a wonder, so gentle, so affectionate, and so clever!

The horse-tamer at 'The Ranch' – a skilled braider – made him a little halter that was a marvel, a truly exquisite lacework of strips of tan leather and, little by little, the other farm-hands, either out of affection for Mario or out of rivalry with the trainer, made all the rest of the accessories, until he had a complete little riding outfit that was admired by 'everyone'.

To Mario he was the finest colt there was, and the most beautiful future race-horse the world had ever seen – and so firm was his conviction in this respect that the taunts of his brother Leo, who persisted in calling the sorrel colt 'jackass' and other such fine names, struck him as veritable blasphemies.

On the other hand, when the foreman of 'The Ranch' said, after sizing up the colt through half-closed eyes:

'In my opinion, he'll be a real beauty, that one' – to Mario

[1] A fence comprising a thorny hedge often interwoven with barbed wire.

the foreman seemed the most likeable and most intelligent of men.

III

Mario's father wanted to start a garden on the grounds adjoining 'The Ranch', and it happened that the 'hateful colt' – which is what some now called him, including the boy's mother, probably because he had trampled on some of her newborn chicks – seemed bent on opposing the project, judging by the vehemence with which he attacked the tender seedlings whenever he got loose. Mario had been warned from the very beginning not to forget to tie up the colt at night; but it also happened that Mario forgot that he had forgotten so many times already, until at last, one morning, his father, exasperated, said to him, shaking his forefinger emphatically and in rhythm with his words:

'The first day that colt destroys another plant, that very day I'll turn him out into the fields . . .'

'Ooooh! . . . Into the fields! . . . Turn him out into the *fields*! . . .'

Did Mario's father happen to have any idea of what turning him into the fields meant to the boy?

He would have to be eight years old like him, to think the way he thought, and love his sorrel colt the way he loved him, to appreciate the real enormity of the threat.

'The fields! . . . Turn him out into the *fields*! . . .' To Mario the fields were something tempestuous, boundless, and abysmal; putting the colt out there would be as atrocious and inhuman as casting a new born babe into the sea.

No wonder, then, that he was not careless again; or that a whole, long week went by without the sorrel colt inflicting the slightest damage on the most insignificant little flower . . .

IV

At daybreak of a radiant February morning, Mario was lying across his bed with his feet up against the wall, 'confiding' some of his plans for the sorrel colt's bright future to his brother Leo, when his mother unexpectedly entered the bedroom.

'So there you are!' she said, all upset. 'So there you are! Have you seen your colt?'

Mario turned crimson and then pale.

'What? My what, mamma?'

'Your colt got loose in the garden again and destroyed a whole lot of things.'

To Mario it seemed as if the universe were crashing down on top of him.

'But . . . how?' he managed to say. 'But, how? . . .'

'Well, I don't know how,' his mother answered, 'but you can't say I haven't warned you time and time again! . . . Now your father . . .'

'But I did tie him up . . . I *did* tie him up . . .'

And as Mario hurriedly got dressed, his hands shook, and he saw everything blurred, as if that room were filling up with smoke.

V

It was a real disaster. Never had the colt dared do so much. This time he had not only trampled the sod of the flower-beds and knocked down with his rump a certain cane trellis over which a vine had started to climb with great elegance, but had carried his mischief to the point of uprooting and pawing with his hoof several rare carnation plants, arranged in an elegant *losange* . . .[1]

'What have you done? What have you done, Baby?'

And as if in a dream, and almost without knowing what he was doing, Mario knelt on the damp ground and began feverishly replanting the flowers while 'Baby', 'the wretch', stood still with his head down, the muzzle of his headstall loose, and a certain air of cynical indifference about his whole 'person'.

VI

Like a sleepwalker, as if treading on a soft wool mattress, Mario led the colt by the halter down the middle of the wide, sloping road lined with towering poplars, which ended there, at the white picket cow-gate which opened on the desolate immensity of the wild fields.

How the blood pounded in the child's brain, how he saw things half-obliterated through a fog, and how he still heard his father's awful threat ringing in his ears! . . .

'Take that colt and put him out into the fields!'

[1] Diamond-shaped flower bed.

Mario did not cry because he could not, for his throat was
in the grip of a steel claw. He walked like an automaton, so
strangely, in fact, that only his mother noticed from the
patio . . .

It was that for Mario, the other side of that cow-gate was
the end of everything; it was the whirlpool where in a few
seconds he and all existence would sink down fatally after the
sorrel colt . . .

When Mario had gone halfway there, his mother could
stand it no longer and moaned, nervously clutching his
father's arm.

'Enough, Juan, enough,' she said.

'All right! . . . Call him! . . .'

But just as Leo started out swiftly, the mother uttered a
sharp cry and the father broke into a frantic run.

There, beside the cow-gate, Mario, with his canvas apron,
had just fallen on the grass, like a gentle bird hit by a bullet . . .

VII

. . . A few days later, when Mario could at last sit up in bed,
his parents, laughing, but with their eyelids red and their
faces pale from the long vigils, ushered the sorrel colt into the
bedroom, pulling him by the halter and pushing on his
rump . . .

BENITO LYNCH

THE CHILD'S VISION

Mr Hubble

I remember Mr Hubble as a tough high-shouldered stooping
old man, of sawdusty fragrance, with his legs extraordinarily
wide apart: so that in my short days I always saw some miles
of open country between them when I met him coming up the
lane.

CHARLES DICKENS, *Great Expectations*

A Blob of Ink

A blob of ink drips into a
Reflecting mirror
And explodes like an atomic
Bomb, shooting out strange
Objects
Like cave paintings, and
Small lily leaves drift
Out in all directions.
The strange shapes smother
Minute objects which glide in their path.
Slowly small blotches explode
Into a monstrous mushroom ready
To crush small specks
And then its
Enemies are melted away inside its
Visible body then overcome
By the magic mirror.
Now the monster turns invisible,
Ready to strike again from its
Ghostly tomb.

MELVYN BRODERICK, aged 11

E

Children's Games

I

This is a schoolyard
crowded
with children

of all ages near a village
on a small stream
mcandering by

where some boys
are swimming
bare-ass

or climbing a tree in leaf
everything
is motion

elder women are looking
after the small
fry

a play wedding a
christening
nearby one leans

hollering
into
an empty hogshead

II

Little girls
whirling their skirts about
until they stand out flat

tops pinwheels
to run in the wind with
or a toy in 3 tiers to spin

with a piece
of twine to make it go
blindman's-buff follow the

leader stilts
high and low tipcat jacks
bowls hanging by the knees

standing on your head
run the gauntlet
a dozen on their backs

feet together kicking
through which a boy must pass
roll the hoop or a

construction
made of bricks
some mason has abandoned

W. CARLOS WILLIAMS

Playing Rugby

He crept about from point to point on the fringe of his line,
making little runs now and then. But his hands were bluish
with cold. He kept his hands in the side pockets of his belted
grey suit. That was a belt round his pocket. And belt was also
to give a fellow a belt. One day a fellow said to Cantwell:
– I'd give you such a belt in a second.
Cantwell had answered:
– Go and fight your match. Give Cecil Thunder a belt. I'd
like to see you. He'd give you a toe in the rump for yourself.
That was not a nice expression. His mother had told him
not to speak with the rough boys in the college. Nice mother!
The first day in the hall of the castle when she had said good-
bye she had put up her veil double to her nose to kiss him:
and her nose and eyes were red. But he had pretended not to
see that she was going to cry. She was a nice mother but she
was not so nice when she cried. And his father had given him
two fiveshilling pieces for pocket money. And his father had
told him if he wanted anything to write home to him and,

whatever he did, never to peach[1] on a fellow. Then at the door of the castle the rector had shaken hands with his father and mother, his soutane[2] fluttering in the breeze, and the car had driven off with his father and mother on it. They cried to him from the car, waving their hands:

—Goodbye, Stephen, goodbye!

—Goodbye, Stephen, goodbye!

He was caught in the whirl of a scrimmage and, fearful of the flashing eyes and muddy boots, bent down to look through the legs. The fellows were struggling and groaning and their legs were rubbing and kicking and stamping. Then Jack Lawton's yellow boots dodged out the ball and all the other boots and legs ran after. He ran after them a little way and then stopped. It was useless to run on. Soon they would be going home for the holidays. After supper in the study hall he would change the number pasted up inside his desk from seventy-seven to seventy-six.

JAMES JOYCE, A Portrait of the Artist as a Young Man

Off to school

'It's about Johnny,' Amy said. 'He's a little young for boarding school at six, but we couldn't take him back to India for two years. It wouldn't be worth it.'

'It's getting him to Paddington,' Bill says. 'Nurse was going to do it. And then we thought of sending him with an outside porter.'

'Of course, there'll be a master to meet him there.'

All this a preface to a request which, after all, is not made. Bill and Amy, either from modesty or pride, we never decided which, are both of them extremely averse from asking any kind of favour.

'And we were just wondering –' Amy says.

'He wouldn't be a nuisance,' Bill assures me. 'He was a bit upset at first when we told him that he had to stay behind. But he's pulled up his socks in the last day or two. Poor little devil. He knows there's no getting out of it.'

I say with mild sarcasm, that if this is all that's troubling them, I should be delighted to take the boy to Paddington.

---

[1] Tell, tell tales, inform against.

[2] A priest's cassock.

They overwhelm me with thanks. Sarcasm has no more effect on them than rain on a couple of tortoises.

'If you *did* have time,' Amy says, 'you might perhaps give him a meringue. He's very fond of meringues. But really, Tom, it's a scandal to waste your time.'

'Whist,' Bill says. 'There he is. Not a word.' And John dashes up with the paper. 'Good lad, record time.' But the boy's haste is obviously to return to them. Amy waves her left-hand fingers in the air and says, 'I'd better have that, Johnny. Your father'll want it in the train.' Johnny puts the paper into the hand, which firmly grips it under the baby.

The porter comes to report all the heavy luggage aboard. Amy and Bill turn to the hand luggage, and find that Loftus has been eating the labels.

'I said he was up to something,' Bill cries, carrying the child like a sheep, hanging down between his hands.

Amy, not yet distracted, murmurs, 'Never mind. It's flour paste.'

'But what about the luggage –'

'Put him in with it – it will keep him quiet.'

Bill thrusts Loftus into the train, who, with a filthy face, and pieces of label sticking to his mouth, chin and cheeks, looks at us still with angelic eyes, while a porter throws the hand luggage up on the rack. Amy and Bill count together, 'One – two – three – four.' 'And the lunch basket,' Bill says. While Amy counts five.

The guard is blowing his whistle. Bill says to me, 'Good-bye, old chap, and remember we mustn't let Edward [brother of Bill and the narrator] down.' Amy kisses me, warmly and unexpectedly, and murmurs, 'You won't forget the meringue.'

I cannot think what she means, till I see that both she and Bill are smiling at the boy. 'Good-bye, old chap.' Bill shakes the child's hand. 'And don't forget to write to your mother.' Amy hands the baby to Bill, lifts John up and kisses him on both cheeks. She is still smiling, but her eyes and nose turn scarlet and tears suddenly appear on her cheeks. She hastily climbs into the train, and Bill hands her the baby, which at once wakes up and utters a loud cry. The train moves, and Bill dives through the door. I see Amy saying something behind the window. But I hear only the baby's screams and an affected voice beside me calling, 'Good-bye, Moms, my love to Paris.'

Probably Amy has been reminding me about the meringue. The train has gone, leaving an empty hole at which both John and I gaze. Then I take the boy's hand and lead him to the station hotel. To my relief, he does not cry. I say, imitating Bill's cheerful address, 'Well, old chap, that's over. Would you like something – a meringue?'

The boy, to my surprise, shakes his head.

'Oh, but I'm sure you'd like a meringue – a double one. They have wonderful meringues here.'

He shakes his head again. I notice that he is trembling all over, his lips, his hands, his knees, even his body. His face is extremely white, and he opens his eyes with a look of amazement, as if he perceives something incredible.

I take him to a cab and we drive to Paddington. He sits quiet; and I think, 'He's being brave, thank goodness. I'd better let him alone.'

.   .   .   .   .

Suddenly . . . I say to him in an encouraging voice, 'So you're going to a boarding school. You'll like that very much. It's a very happy time.'

He shakes his head.

'I liked it. I thought I shouldn't like it, but I really enjoyed it quite well.'

I see to my horror that tears are trickling down his cheeks. He cries like his mother with stoic face. And after a little reflection I encourage him, 'Don't cry, old chap.'

'I'm not crying,' he says in a low voice, 'it's my eyes.'

We are at Paddington. But no master accosts us. The boy, thank heaven, has stopped weeping. I say hopefully, 'Just time for something – a cream cake, or what about a cup of chocolate?'

'No thank you, uncle.'

He disengages his hand from mine, and I look down to see if I have given him offence. But he looks up at me with a face which startles me by its perfect comprehension of my course of feeling. He says, 'The master will be coming.' He means 'Perhaps I'd better not be holding hands when this envoy from the unknown world of exile comes upon us.'

The master arrives. He is a short hook-nosed man with a friendly manner. He taps John on the head and calls him young feller – he beams at me and says loudly, 'The worst is over, I see.'

I can feel, rather than see, the expression on the child's face as he hears this; and I can feel the sense of loneliness and smallness intensified within him, by words which mean, 'These small animals needn't be taken too seriously.' I feel for the child, but I cannot think what to do or what to say to him. The master waits a moment, looks encouragingly at us both, then at his watch. He remarks, 'We've five minutes. What about a bun, young feller?'

The boy shakes his head and says, 'Good-bye, uncle.'

'Good-bye, my dear.' I offer him half a crown. He takes it, and says nothing, not even thank you. The master, to my surprise, turns his back, and at once the child puts out his arms and reaches upwards. I understand his motive in time to stoop. He embraces me and whispers in a voice which already seems to come from a distance, 'Good-bye, uncle. Thank you most awfully for everything.' Probably a formula taught him by his mother, for use after parties.

Then he is walking away with the tactful master. I notice a half crown lying on the pavement, but I do not realize that the boy has dropped it until I am several yards away. And when I return for it, it has already disappeared. Someone of the group of porters and loungers standing opposite has picked it up, and when I look at them several of them stare back at me, with those wooden faces which say, 'Think what you like – you can't do anything.' I feel again a deep oppression of weakness, as if the whole of the civilized order about me, in which Bill and Amy walk so confidently and so rashly, and the young John carries his grief with so much dignity, is nothing but an appearance, a dream. And from the dream, our unhappy people, especially Bill, Amy, etc., are about to be awakened.

JOYCE CAREY, *To be a Pilgrim*

The Rainbow-Bird [1]

All afternoon as she bent over her slate, Maggie's mind had been filled with a vision of the bird. Blue-green shot with gold, its tail an arrow. Her hair fell over her intense, grape-dark eyes; she hardly knew what she was writing. It was the

[1] The bee-eater.

same every day now. The hands crawled down the cracked face of the clock with aggravated slowness; the teacher's voice droned on and on like a blowfly against the windowpane; the other children squirmed in their seats and folded paper darts to throw across the room. But all she lived for was the moment when she would see again the coloured shape skim from its cavern in the earth, making her catch her breath as if its wings had brushed across her heart.

As soon as school was out she flashed a look at Don, racing down to the bottom fence along through the bushes that covered the side of the hill. Don was a little behind, limping because of his sore toe; flushed and breathless Maggie had reached the bottom of the gully before he emerged from the undergrowth. One stocking had fallen over her ankle and her hat was at the back of her neck, held by the elastic around her throat, but she cared for nothing but getting away.

From the bottom of the playground she could hear the other girls calling her.

'Wait on, Maggie! We're coming, too.'

She tried to shut their voices from her ears. None of them must find out her secret. She hated their empty faces, their coldly-mocking eyes; they made fun of her because she carried beetles' wings and cowries about in her matchbox to stare at under the desk.

'Come on, Don,' she called back impatiently, 'they'll all be on us soon.'

He growled as he caught up with her.

'It's all right for you – you got boots on. This prickly grass hurts like blazes. Why didn't you go down the road?'

'This is nearly half-a-mile shorter . . . Come on.'

They panted up the other hill and across a cleared paddock that lay between them and the beach. Before the eyes of both of them was the deep cleft left by the store-truck when it was bogged months before, and the little round hole with a heap of sand in front of it. Such a tiny tunnel in the side of the rut that no one would notice unless he saw the bird fly out. They had come on it together when they were looking for mushrooms; there had been a sudden burr of wings almost beneath their feet, a shimmer of opal in the sunbright air, and then a stillness as the bird settled on the she-oak[1] thirty

---

[1] An evergreen tree with drooping feathery branches. Some species grow in Cornwall and the Scillies. Its timber has prominent much valued medullary rays.

yards away, making their hearts turn over with the sheer
beauty of its bronze and luminous green.

A rainbow-bird! And it had come from that rounded tunnel
in the sandy earth where the couch-grass was growing over
the old rut. Don had wanted to put his hand in and feel if
there were any young ones, but Maggie had caught his arm,
her eyes desperate.

'No, don't! She's watching. She'll go away and never come
back – never.'

She wanted just to stand and let her eyes have their fill.
That stretch of cropped turf, with the she-oak on a sandy rise
above the beach and the miraculous bird shining out of the
greeny-grey branches! It was only rarely they surprised her in
the nest, for she usually seemed to feel the pattering vibration
of their feet along the ground and slip out unobserved. But
they never had to look far for her. There in the she-oak she
shone, flame-bright and radiant, as if she had just dropped
from the blue sky. And sometimes they saw her mate
skimming through the air after flies, taking long, sweeping
curves and pausing at the top of the curve, a skater on wings,
a maker of jewelled patterns, body light as thistledown, every
feather blazing with fire and colour. The vision came back to
Maggie each night before she closed her eyes in sleep. It
belonged to a different world from the school, the dusty road,
the yard behind the store that was filled with rusty tins and
broken cases.

'That girl!' her mother said, hearing her mutter on the
pillow. 'It's a bird now.'

They hurried across the road, past the spindled-legged
house with no fence around it, past the red-roofed cottage
where there were bathing-suits hung out to dry. Surely this
afternoon the little birds would be out in front of the nest!
The day before when they had lain with their ears close to the
ground they had heard something thin but distinct, a cheeping
and twittering. It had come to them through the warm earth,
thrilling them with intense life. Those bits of living colour
down there in the dark – how wonderful it would be when
they came out into the light!

Maggie pulled up suddenly in the final run, clutching at
Don's arm.

'Wait! . . . Someone's there . . . Don't go on yet.'

Breathing hard, Don stood staring at the big, dark figure

on the slope overlooking the sea.

'It's Peter Riley watching if the mullet are coming in.'

'No, it isn't. It's Cafferty. I know his hat.'

'Cafferty?'

'Yes, Cafferty the Honey Man.'

The man was standing almost on the nest, looking down into the she-oak by the beach, his body still as a wooden stump, his eyes intent as their own. He moved slightly to the right; they saw he had a gun at his side. Horror laid an icy hand on the girl's heart. What was he doing with a gun there?

Suddenly she started to run.

'Come on! I believe he's found the nest. I believe . . .'

Her slim legs twinkled like beams of light over the turf, her print frock blew up over her heated face, and Don found it hard to keep up with her. She was out of breath when she reached Cafferty and her eyes were points of fire. He was too occupied to notice her; he was shifting the gun in his hands and watching the she-oak tree. She saw a lump in the pocket of his shirt, a stain of blood.

Words came thickly from her throat.

'What're you doing with that gun?'

'Eh?' he said, hardly looking round.

'You – you've been shooting something . . . What's that in your pocket?'

Cafferty let his eyes rest on her stolidly, a slow grin parting his lips.

'Guess.'

'It's not . . . It's a bird.'

'Right. Right, first shot. Most peopl'd have thought it was a rabbit . . . Ever see one of those coloured bee-eaters, little girl? Her mate's somewhere about. I'll get him too, before long.'

He took the crumpled bird from his pocket and dangled it before her proudly. Through a blur she saw the ruffled bronze and emerald of its plumage, the film over its eyes, the drop of blood oozing from its beak. Then she threw herself on the turf.

'Beast! That's what you are . . . A b-beast.'

Cafferty looked from her small, sobbing figure to that of the boy, a sheepish bewilderment in his eyes. He was a hulking, slow-witted fellow, who lived in a humpy[1] on the

_____
[1] A native Australian hut or a very small primitive hut erected by settlers.

other side of the creek, surrounded by his hives and a thick growth of tea-tree.

'What's the trouble?' he asked. 'That bird is it?'

Don had no reply. He was confused, half-ashamed of his sister.

'Lord, you don't want to worry about vermin like that,' said Cafferty. 'Death on bees, them things are – hanging round the hives and licking 'em up as they come out. And they're not satisfied with robbing you like that, the little devils; they'll go through a flying swarm and take out the queen. It's a fact. Dinkum . . . I'd like to wipe the lot of 'em off the face of the earth.'

He went over to the tiny opening of the tunnel and bruised the soft earth down over the face of it with his heavy boot. There was a dull passion in his absorbed eyes, a sense of warring against evil.

'No, you don't want to trouble about the likes of them. Unless it's to go after them with a shanghai[1]. There's sixpence a head waiting for any you fetch me. Tell the other youngsters that – a tanner a head. I'm going to clear the lot of 'em out this winter.'

Shouldering his gun he moved off down the beach, a lumbering heaviness on his gait. Maggie was still stretched prone on the turf, her face in her arms, and Don watched her awhile, awkward and ill-at-ease. But the superiority of one who has not given himself away was slowly asserting itself. Picking up the dead bird that Cafferty had thrown on the grass he fingered it clumsily, wondering if there were any bees in its crop. It was still warm, but its plumage was ruffled and streaky, and it didn't look nearly so wonderful as when it had shot into the air, the light on its wings. Death on bees, the Honey Man had said. He began to feel a contempt for it.

'Come on, Mag! He's gone now. And the other kids'll be coming along soon.'

She rose from the grass, tossing back her hair and looking at the bird with reddened eyes.

'Chuck it away.'

'Why? I'm going to take it home and skin it.'

'Chuck it away!' she stormed.

He hesitated a moment, and then obeyed her. They trailed

[1]A catapult.

over the grass towards the store, Don swinging his bag and whistling to show he didn't care. There must be a lot of rainbow birds about, and if the Honey Man kept his promise . . . Sixpence a head! He could go out with the other boys on Saturday mornings, looking all along the sandy banks. But he wouldn't use a shanghai – no fear! His new Bayard[1] was three times as good.

Maggie took no more notice of him than if he were merely a shadow behind her. Their father was standing waiting for them at the bowser[2] outside the store, and Don had to go for orders on his pony. Maggie trudged upstairs to the room over the shop and flung herself down on the bed. Darkness had fallen over her life. Whenever she closed her eyes she could see the Honey Man's evil face, the broken, tobacco-stained teeth revealed in a grin through the ragged growth of beard. Hatred welled up in her as she thought of him squatting among the tea-tree[3] on the other side of the creek, his gun between his knees, his eyes watching the leaves above. Devil! Grinning devil! If only forked lightning would leap out of the sky and char him to ashes.

When the evening meal was over she went upstairs again without waiting to do her homework. Her mother's voice followed at a distance, dying behind the closed door:

'What's the matter with Maggie now? . . . The way that girl lets herself get worked up.'

Lying awake, Maggie tried to imagine herself running down the slope and stopping suddenly to see the rainbow-bird whirling round over three spots of colour on the grass. But no! She could only see the soft earth around the nest, squashed by the Honey Man's boot, and the dead bird lying on the grass with a drop of blood on its beak. Wonder and magic – they had gone out of everything! And Don was swaggering round, pretending he didn't care.

A light rain had begun to fall, making hardly any sound upon the roof, dropping with a faint insistent tinkle into the tanks. There were people coming and going in the store below. Between broken drifts of sleep she heard voices running on and on, the telephone's muffled burring, the

[1] Make of gun.
[2] A petrol pump.
[3] The shrub or trees of the myrtle family. Its leaves have been used as a substitute for tea.

occasional hoot of a car. But all noises were muted, coming through a pad of distance, of woolly darkness. A funeral, she thought vaguely. They were burying the rainbow-bird.

Near morning, or so it seemed, she heard someone come upstairs, and there was a blare of light in her eyes. Her mother was bending over her with a candle.

'Not asleep yet, dear? Have those people kept you awake?'

The drowsy aftermath of feeling made Maggie's voice thick.

'N-no; it wasn't that. It wasn't that. It was because . . . Why do they all come here now?'

Her mother tucked an end of the quilt in.

'They brought Mr Cafferty to the shop to wait for the ambulance. He had a little accident and had to be taken in to the hospital . . . Go to sleep now.'

Maggie's eyes were wide open.

'He's dead?'

'Good gracious, no! Nothing to worry about. He must have been dragging the gun after him as he climbed through the wire-fence across the creek, but they found him soon after it happened. Only in the thigh the wound was.'

Through Maggie's mind flashed a sudden conviction.

'He will die. I know he will. . . . Serve him right, too.'

'You don't understand what you're talking about, child,' said her mother in a formal shocked voice. 'Everyone's fond of the Honey Man and hopes he'll be all right soon . . . You've been lying awake too long. Go to sleep now.'

She faded away, leaving Maggie to stare up at the ceiling in the dark. But the vision of a world oppressed by a heavy, brutal heel had vanished. Her mind was lit up again; everything had come right. She could see the cropped slope by the sea, the over-grown wheel-rut, the small, round tunnel with the heap of sand in front of it. And it was the man with the gun who was lying crumpled on the grass. Above him sailed the rainbow-bird, lustrous, triumphant, her opal body poised at the top of a curve, shimmering in the sunbright air.

VANCE PALMER, *The Rainbow Bird and Other Stories*

'TYGER! TYGER!'

The Tyger

Tyger! Tyger! burning bright
In the forests of the night,
What immortal hand or eye
Could frame thy fearful symmetry?

In what distant deeps or skies
Burnt the fire of thine eyes?
On what wings dare he aspire?
What the hand dare seize the fire?

And what shoulder, & what art,
Could twist the sinews of thy heart?
And when thy heart began to beat,
What dread hand? & what dread feet?

What the hammer? what the chain?
In what furnace was thy brain?
What the anvil? what dread grasp
Dare its deadly terrors clasp?

When the stars threw down their spears,
And water'd heaven with their tears,
Did he smile his work to see?
Did he who made the Lamb make thee?

Tyger! Tyger! burning bright
In the forests of the night,
What immortal hand or eye,
Dare frame thy fearful symmetry?

WILLIAM BLAKE

To see the Rabbit

We are going to see the rabbit.
We are going to see the rabbit.
Which rabbit, people say?
Which rabbit, ask the children?
Which rabbit?
The only rabbit,
The only rabbit in England,
Sitting behind a barbed-wire fence
Under the floodlights, neon lights,
Sodium lights,
Nibbling grass
On the only patch of grass
In England, in England
(Except the grass by the hoardings
Which doesn't count)
We are going to see the rabbit
And we must be there on time.

First we shall go by escalator,
Then we shall go by underground,
And then we shall go by motorway,
And then by helicopterway,
And the last ten yards we shall have to go
On foot.

And now we are going
All the way to see the rabbit,
We are nearly there,
We are longing to see it,

And so is the crowd
Which is here in thousands
With mounted policemen
And big loudspeakers
And bands and banners,
And everyone has come a long way.

But soon we shall see it
Sitting and nibbling
The blades of grass
On the only patch of grass
In – but something has gone wrong!
Why is everyone so angry
Why is everyone so jostling
And slanging and complaining?

The rabbit has gone,
Yes, the rabbit has gone.
He has actually burrowed down into the earth
And made himself a warren, under the earth,
Despite all these people,
And what shall we do?
What *can* we do?

It is all a pity, you must be disappointed,
Go home and do something else for today,
Go home again, go home for today.
For you cannot hear the rabbit under the earth
Remarking rather sadly to himself, by himself,
As he rests in his warren, under the earth:
'It won't be long, they are bound to come,
They are bound to come and find me, even here.'

ALAN BROWNJOHN

Lament for Prytherch

When I was young, when I was young!
Were you ever young, Prytherch, a rich farmer:
Cows in the byre, sheep in the pen,
A brown egg under each hen,
The barns oozing corn like honey?
You are old now; time's geometry
Upon your face by which we tell
Your sum of years has with sharp care

Conspired and crossed your brow with grief.
Your heart that is dry as a dead leaf
Undone by frost's cruel chemistry
Clings in vain to the bare bough
Where once in April a bird sang.

R. S. THOMAS

A Night Watch

As silently as its shadow an owl flew over the farm garth[1]; its wings seemed to be part of the air, and the shadow itself rippled over the stones, startling the mice.

Adam saw the shadow on the grass and as it climbed the white wire net. The vixen saw it from beyond the wall. There was no movement from the hen run: the fox turned to go. Then she came round again, through the sheep gate, and round to the back of the farm. Adam heard nothing and saw nothing. He stretched his fingers one at a time, and yawned, trying to stretch the beginnings of sleep out of his eyes. But though he dismissed it, again the music of sleep began sounding in his ears. The owl called: he heard it as a trumpet; a cockchafer whirred in the still air: he heard it as a drum; against his ear an ivy leaf moved under a spider: he heard in it the soft song of treble violins.

Then in a start he woke at once, still hearing music, but it was only Lew Gill lapping against the lonely water-stones. He was awake now, and the cold moon burnt coldly like frost on his hands and head.

Something stood in the field: black shape and black shadow. The vixen looked at the wire, and turned to go back the way she had come.

[1] Enclosure, yard, garden, paddock.

'I should shoot,' thought Adam. Though his hand touched the gun, it did not want to pick it up and raise it in sudden movement. He watched the fox as if she were on a stage. She walked over the grass like a dancer: each leg had its attendant pointing shadow; the Gill still made rippling music. The fox made her own ballet, pointing each silent foot, and reached the shadow of the wall.

Under the tractor shed the moonlight moved: a straight gleam pointed to the fox; the night burst round the moving moonlight: twice there was thunder in the air; the fells sent the double report back from bank to bank and scar to scar. Every creature that heard crouched low and fearful; but one crouched animal heard nothing: shot moves faster than sound, and the fox was dead before she fell.

Adam saw his gun standing beside him, and knew he had not fired. 'Good,' he said. 'Oh good,' because he had looked at the fox with joy: as if it were a favourite dog or any dear beautiful thing.

Mr Owland stood up. Adam stood up, and the cold air bit into all the warm folds of his skin. He and Mr Owland stood over the fox.

'Did you do it, or did I?' said Mr Owland.

'You did,' said Adam.

'Oh, damn,' said Mr Owland. 'Why should I?'

'I'm glad I didn't,' said Adam. They looked down at the animal lying on the shadow of the wall.

'A vixen,' said Mr Owland. 'I think she's finished feeding her cubs: they'll be eating meat now. I shall have to watch for them in the autumn: they won't go far from here until they're hungry.'

'I think I went to sleep,' said Adam.

'I wish I had,' said Mr Owland. 'We'd better bury her now. Don't touch: she'll be covered with fleas.'

He went back to the tractor shed to find two mattocks and a crowbar, and a length of cord to pull the dead vixen with: a fox has a very strong smell that hangs on you if you touch. Mr Owland came back with the clattering tools, hitched the string round the fox's hind leg, and dragged her behind him into the middle of the field.

They started to dig. Mrs Owland came out in her dressing-gown to see what was happening.

'Oh, did you get one?' she said. 'Who did it?'

'I did,' said Mr Owland. 'First shot, behind the ear, and the second in the same place. Has Mary anything to say?'

'She's gone in with Nan,' said Mrs Owland. 'They're having a fight: they'll settle down soon.'

'Tell her it was an ugly savage great grandmother fox,' said Mr Owland. 'One that would have died in the winter in any case.'

'She'll forget about it if she doesn't see it,' said Mrs Owland. 'I'll get you a pot of tea ready.'

'Good. Hang these stones. Where's the crowbar?'

Digging a fox's grave was a quicker job than making post-holes: the shape could be anything, and the hole need not be so deep. The damp stones came up shining in the moonlight, and the hole went down velvet dark.

'Enough,' said Mr Owland. 'Let's put her in.' He dragged the fox in, and let her lie, then put the stones over her, and filled the hole.

'Altogether,' he said, 'a fox is a better animal than a hen. But no one can do anything about that. Hens lay eggs: foxes don't.'

Ten minutes later the field was empty. The moon looked down on a little mound of stone and soil. The little foxes in the fell waited and watched. But they were awake in vain.

WILLIAM MAYNE, *A Grass Rope*

THE WRITER'S MOTIVES

'TELL 'EM WHAT HAPPENED'

Dempsey v. Firpo

Alan Gould, the former executive editor of the Associated Press, has described his quandary as a young sports reporter covering the Dempsey-Firpo fight in 1922. Dempsey knocked Firpo to the floor seven times in the first round, then Firpo bounced Dempsey out of the ring. Dempsey returned and knocked Firpo unconscious. Gould sat motionless at his typewriter, unable to think of the vivid verbs and adjectives he thought he needed to describe the most action-packed fight in boxing history. Pop Byers, a veteran reporter for the New York *Sun*, sensed Gould's problem, leaned over to him and said, 'Alan, just tell 'em what happened.' Gould never forgot the advice.

WILLIAM L. RIVERS, *The Mass Media*

Undersea Operation

'They are giving him ether now,' was what they said back in the aft torpedo rooms.

'He's gone under and they're getting ready to cut him open,' the crew whispered, sitting on their pipe bunks cramped between torpedoes.

One man went forward and put his arm quietly around the shoulders of another man who was handling the bow diving planes. 'Keep her steady, Jake,' he said. 'They've just made the first cut. They're feeling around for it now.'

'They' were a little bunch of anxious-faced men with their arms thrust into reversed white pajama coats. Gauze bandages hid all their expressions except the tensity in their eyes.

'It' was an acute appendix inside Dean Rector of Chautauqua, Kan. The stabbing pains had become unendurable the day before, which was Rector's first birthday at sea. He was nineteen.

The big depth gauge that looks like a factory clock and stands beside the 'Christmas tree' of red and green gauges regulating the flooding chambers showed where they were.

They were below the surface. And above them – and below them, too – were enemy waters crossed and recrossed by whirring propellers of Japanese destroyers, transports, and submarines.

The nearest naval surgeon competent to operate on the young seaman was thousands of miles and many days away. There was just one way to prevent the appendix from bursting and that was for the crew to operate upon their shipmate themselves.

And that's what they did: they operated upon him. It was probably one of the largest operations in numbers of participants that ever occurred.

'He says he's ready to take the chance,' the gobs whispered from bulkhead to bulkhead.

'That guy's regular' – the word travelled from bow planes to propeller and back again.

They kept her steady.

The chief surgeon was a twenty-three-year-old pharmacist's mate wearing a blue blouse with white-taped collar and a squashy white duck cap. His name was Wheeler B. Lipes.

It took Lipes in his flap-finger gloves nearly twenty minutes to find the appendix.

'I have tried one side of the caecum,' he whispered after the first few minutes. 'Now I'm trying the other.'

Whispered bulletins seeped back into the engine room and crew's quarters.

'The doc has tried one side of something and now is trying the other.'

After more search, Lipes finally whispered, 'I think I've got it. It's curled way up behind the blind gut.'

Lipes was using the classical McBurney's incision. Now was the time when his shipmate's life was completely in his hands.

'Two more spoons.' (Bent metal spoons were used as surgical retractors.) They passed the word to Lt Ward.

'Two spoons at 1445 hours,' wrote Skipper Ferrall on his notepad.

'More flashlights. And another battle lantern,' demanded Lipes.

The patient's face, lathered with white petrolatum, began to grimace.

'Give him some more ether,' ordered the doctor.

Hoskins looked doubtfully at the original five pounds of ether, now sunken to hardly three quarters of one can. But once again the tea-strainer was soaked in ether. The fumes mounted, thickening the ward-room air and making the operating staff giddy.

'Want those blowers speeded up?' the captain asked the doc.

The blowers began to whir louder.

Suddenly came the moment when the doc reached out his hand, pointing toward the needle threaded with twenty-day chromic catgut.

One by one the sponges came out. One by one the table-spoons bent into right angles were withdrawn and returned to the galley. At the end it was the skipper who nudged Lipes and pointed to the tally of bent tablespoons. One was missing. Lipes reached into the incision for the last time and withdrew the wishbone spoon and closed the incision . . .

GEORGE WELLER, *Undersea Operation*

SATIRE

The Superintendent

In due course the superintendent stood up in front of the pulpit, with a closed hymn-book in his hand and his fore-finger inserted between its leaves, and commanded attention. When a Sunday-school superintendent makes his customary little speech, a hymn book in the hand is as necessary as is the inevitable sheet of music in the hand of a singer who stands forward on the platform and sings a solo at a concert – though why is a mystery; for neither the hymn-book nor the sheet of music is ever referred to by the sufferer. This superintendent was a slim creature of thirty-five, with a sandy goatee, and short sandy hair; he wore a stiff standing-collar whose upper edge almost reached his ears, and whose sharp points curved forward abreast the corners of his mouth – a fence that compelled a straight lookout ahead, and a turning of the whole body when a side view was required. His chin was propped on a spreading cravat, which was as broad and as long as a bank-note, and had fringed ends; his boot toes were turned sharply up, in the fashion of the day, like sleigh-runners – an effect patiently and laboriously produced by the young men by sitting with their toes pressed against a wall for hours together. Mr Walters was very earnest of m n, and very sincere and honest at heart; and he held sacred things and places in such reverence, and so separated them from worldly matters, that unconsciously to himself his Sunday-school voice had acquired a peculiar intonation which was wholly absent on week-days. He began after this fashion:

'Now, children, I want you all to sit up just as straight and pretty as you can, and give me all your attention for a minute or two. There, that is it. That is the way good little boys and girls should do. I see one little girl who is looking out of the window – I am afraid she thinks I am out there somewhere – perhaps up in one of the trees making a speech to the little birds. [Applausive titter.] I want to tell you how good it makes me feel to see so many bright, clean little faces assembled in a place like this, learning to do right and be good.'

And so forth, and so on. It is not necessary to set down the rest of the oration. It was of a pattern which does not vary, and so it is familiar to us all.

MARK TWAIN, *Tom Sawyer*

MOODS

The Thing

He struck flame and transferred it to the waxen tip.

He crouched in his flickering tent. His unfocussed eyes found places on his legs where the flesh was torn.

He sat turning himself back into Smithers[1] as he was before this had left him unaltered, forming plans.

[1] Smithers, a reporter, is down a coal mine. He has been trying to imagine that he is a hero but, feeling terrified, he realizes he is only himself after all.

Then stopped breathing.

His echo breathed on, then stopped in its interval.

But there was another breath. The whole rock was breathing, furring its pulse in blood-red panic. A sound was scratching towards him.

He stilled fingers, boot-clickings, teeth, all his chattering bone, and saw beyond the fringe of light a humped shape moving up on him, scuffing so slightly and tortoising closer. He panted aloud and his hand sought stone. It was his Horror from childhood, the Crawler, Death, the Fingering Beast, it was the midnight spectre at the back of his mirror, the long-legged hunch-backed worm of the cave: a round prehistoric head with a single proboscing eye came goggling into his panic and he smashed it away with rock. Then the candle was out and the Thing wrestled at him, sprawling over and over in shale of that cinderous dark.

MICHAEL BALDWIN, *Underneath*

Darkness

It was silent and dark, and the children were afraid.[1] They huddled together, their backs to an outcrop of rock. Far below them, in the bed of the gully, a little stream flowed inland –

[1] Mary and her brother are the only survivors of an aircraft which has just crashed in the Australian desert.

soon to peter out in the vastness of the Australian desert.
Above them the walls of the gully climbed smoothly to a
moonless sky.

The little boy nestled more closely against his sister. He
was trembling.

She felt for his hand, and held it, very tightly.

'All right, Peter,' she whispered. 'I'm here.'

She felt the tension ebb slowly out of him, the trembling
die gradually away. When a boy is only eight a big sister of
thirteen can be wonderfully comforting.

'Mary,' he whispered, 'I'm hungry. Let's have something to
eat.'

The girl sighed. She felt in the pocket of her frock, and
pulled out a paper-covered stick of barley sugar. It was their
last one. She broke it, gave him half, and slipped the other
half back in her pocket.

'Don't bite,' she whispered. 'Suck.'

Why they were whispering they didn't know. Perhaps
because everything was so very silent: like a church. Or was it
because they were afraid; afraid of being heard?

For a while the only sounds were the distant rippling of
water over stone, and the sucking of lips round a diminishing
stick of barley sugar. Then the boy started to fidget, moving
restlessly from one foot to another. Again the girl reached for
his hand.

'Aren't you comfy, Pete?'

'No.'

'What is it?'

'My leg's bleeding again. I can feel the wet.'

She bent down. The handkerchief that she had tied round
his thigh was now draped like a recalcitrant garter over his
ankle. She refastened it, and they huddled together, holding
hands, looking into the powdery blackness of the Australian
night.

They could see nothing. They could hear nothing – apart
from the lilt of the rivulet – for it was still too early for the
stirring of bush life. Later there'd be other sounds; the hoot of
the mopoke,[1] the mating howl of the dingo, and the leathery
flip-flap-flip of the wings of flying foxes. But now, an hour
after sunset, the bush was silent: frighteningly still: full, to the

---

[1]Various Australian birds, but usually the owl; so-called because of the sound it
makes.

children, of terrors all the greater for being unknown. It was a far cry from here to their comfortable home in Charleston, South Carolina.

The hours meandered past like slow, unhurrying snails. At last the boy's head dropped to his sister's lap. He snuggled closer. His breathing became slower, deeper. He slept.

But the girl didn't sleep; that would never have done; for she had to keep guard. She was the elder. The responsibility was hers. That was the way it had always been, as far back as, she could remember. Always she had been the big sister who had stuck plaster on Peter's knees, had taught him to tie his shoe laces, and had taken the lead in their games of Indians and cowboys. Now that they were lost – somewhere in the middle of an unknown continent – the weight of her responsibility was greater than ever. A wave of tenderness welled up inside her. Always she had big-sistered him; now she must mother him as well.

For a while she sat staring into the darkness; the darkness that was warm, thick and almost tangible; soon her mind became utterly blank. The day's events had been too overwhelming; had drawn on her too heavily. The rhythmic beat of the small boy's slumber came to her lullingly now. Gradually her breathing fell in step with his. The whisper of the creek came to her like the croon of a lullaby. Her eyelids drooped and closed, fluttered and closed again. Soon she too was fast asleep.

In the darkness beyond the gully, the bush came slowly to life.

A lumbering wombat came creeping out of his ground den. His short stumpy body forced a way through the underscrub; his long food-foraging snout ploughing through the sandy earth in search of his favourite roots. Suddenly he stopped: sniffed: his nostrils dilated. He followed the strange new scent. Soon he came to the gully. He looked the children over; thoughtfully, not hungrily, for he was a vegetarian, an eater of roots. His curiosity satisfied, he shambled slowly away.

Random fireflies zigzagged by; their nightlights flickering like sparklets from a roving toy-sized forge.

Soon, creeping along the edge of darkness, came another creature: a marsupial tiger-cat, her eyes widened by the night to glowing oriflammes[1] of fire. She too had scented the children; she too clambered into the gully and looked them over.

[1] Streamers, or little banners of red silk.

They smelt young and tender and tempting; but they were large; too bulky, she decided, to drag back to her mewling litter. On velvet paws she slunk away.

A night mist tried to gather: failed – for the air in the gully was too warm – and dissipated into pre-dawn dew. The dampness settled on the children, pressing down their clothes, tracing the outline of their bodies in tiny globules of pearl. They stirred but didn't wake. They were lost in their dreams.

In her sleep the girl moved uneasily. She was in the aeroplane again, and she knew that something was wrong. She and Peter were the only passengers, sandwiched between the crates of vegetables and the frozen carcasses of beef, and she was watching the port engine, waiting for the flames she knew would come. Too soon they were there; the tiny tongues of red licking out of the cowling. In her sleep she twisted and moaned; then mercifully, her mind went blank – nature's safety valve that protects, even in dreams, those who have been shocked beyond endurance – and the next thing she dreamt was that she and Peter were staggering away from the blazing plane, she pulling him frantically because one of his legs was numb and his feet kept sinking into the soft, yielding sand. 'Quick, Peter,' she gasped. 'Quick, before it explodes.' She heard a dull pulsating roar, and looking back saw the figure of the Navigating Officer carrying the pilot and clambering out of the wreckage. In the heat of the explosion he glowed white-hot, disintegrating. Again her mind went numb, but in her sleep she clutched her brother's hand; clutched it and squeezed it so tight that he half-woke and slid awkwardly off her lap.

The nightlights of the fireflies became pale and anaemic. Out of the east crept a permeating greyness; a pearly opaqueness in the sky; the sun-up of another day.

JAMES VANCE MARSHALL, *Walkabout*

FANTASY

The Last Queen

The Queen led them out of the Hall of Images into a long corridor and then through a whole maze of halls and stairs and courtyards. Again and again they heard parts of the great palace collapsing, sometimes quite close to them. Once a huge arch came thundering down only a moment after they had passed through it. The Queen was walking quickly – the children had to trot to keep up with her – but she showed no sign of fear. Digory thought, 'She's wonderfully brave. And strong. She's what I call a Queen! I do hope she's going to tell us the story of this place.'

She did tell them certain things as they went along:

'That is the door to the dungeons,' she would say, or 'That passage leads to the principal torture chambers,' or 'This was the old banqueting hall where my great-grandfather bade seven hundred nobles to a feast and killed them all before they had drunk their fill. They had rebellious thoughts.'

They came at last into a hall larger and loftier than any they had yet seen. From its size and from the great doors at the far end, Digory thought that now at last they must be coming to the main entrance. In this he was quite right. The doors were dead black, either ebony or some black metal which is not found in our world. They were fastened with great bars, most of them too high to reach and all too heavy to lift. He wondered how they would get out.

The Queen let go of his hand and raised her arm. She drew herself up to her full height and stood rigid. Then she said something which they couldn't understand (but it sounded horrid) and made an action as if she were throwing something towards the doors. And those high and heavy doors trembled for a second as if they were made of silk and then crumbled away till there was nothing left of them but a heap of dust on the threshold.

'Whew!' whistled Digory.

'Has your master magician, your uncle, power like mine?' asked the Queen, firmly seizing Digory's hand again. 'But I shall know later. In the meantime, remember what you have seen. This is what happens to things, and to people, who stand in my way.'

Much more light than they had yet seen in that country was pouring in through the now empty doorway, and when the Queen led them out through it they were not surprised to find themselves in the open air. The wind that blew in their faces was cold, yet somehow stale. They were looking from a high terrace and there was a great landscape spread out below them.

Low down and near the horizon hung a great, red sun, far bigger than our sun. Digory felt at once that it was also older than ours: a sun near the end of its life, weary of looking down upon that world. To the left of the sun, and higher up, there was a single star, big and bright. Those were the only two things to be seen in the dark sky; they made a dismal group. And on the earth, in every direction, as far as the eye could reach, there spread a vast city in which there was no living thing to be seen. And all the temples, towers, palaces, pyramids, and bridges cast long, disastrous-looking shadows in the light of that withered sun. Once a great river had flowed through the city, but the water had long since vanished, and it was now only a wide ditch of grey dust.

'Look well on that which no eyes will ever see again,' said the Queen. 'Such was Charn, that great city, the city of the King of Kings, the wonder of the world, perhaps of all worlds. Does your uncle rule any city as great as this, boy?'

'No,' said Digory. He was going to explain that Uncle Andrew didn't rule any cities, but the Queen went on:

'It is silent now. But I have stood here when the whole air was full of the noises of Charn; the trampling feet, the creaking of wheels, the cracking of whips and the groaning of slaves, the thunder of chariots, and the sacrificial drums beating in the temples. I have stood here (but that was near the end) when the roar of battle went up from every street and the river of Charn ran red.' She paused and added, 'All in one moment one woman blotted it out for ever.'

'Who?' said Digory in a faint voice; but he had already guessed the answer.

'I', said the Queen. 'I, Jadis, the last Queen, but the Queen of the World.'

The two children stood silent, shivering in the cold wind.

'It was my sister's fault,' said the Queen. 'She drove me to it. May the curse of all the Powers rest upon her forever! At any moment I was ready to make peace – yes, and to spare her life too, if only she would yield me the throne. But she would not. Her pride has destroyed the whole world. Even after the war had begun, there was a solemn promise that neither side would use Magic. But when she broke her promise, what could I do? Fool! As if she did not know that I had more Magic than she! She even knew that I had the secret of the Deplorable Word. Did she think – she was always a weakling – that I would not use it?'

'What was it?' said Digory.

'That was the secret of secrets,' said Queen Jadis. 'It had long been known to the great kings of our race that there was a word which, if spoken with the proper ceremonies, would destroy all living things except the one who spoke it. But the ancient kings were weak and soft-hearted and bound themselves and all who should come after them with great oaths never even to seek after the knowledge of that word. But I learned it in a secret place and paid a terrible price to learn it. I did not use it until she forced me to it. I fought and fought to overcome her by every other means. I poured out the blood of my armies like water – '

'Beast!' muttered Polly.

'The last great battle,' said the Queen, 'raged for three days here in Charn itself. For three days I looked down upon it from this very spot. I did not use my power till the last of my soldiers had fallen, and the accursed woman, my sister, at the head of her rebels was halfway up those great stairs that lead up from the city to the terrace. Then I waited till we were so close that we could see one another's faces. She flashed her horrible, wicked eyes upon me and said, "Victory." "Yes," said I, "Victory, but not yours." Then I spoke the Deplorable Word. A moment later I was the only living thing beneath the sun.'

'But the people?' gasped Digory.

'What people, boy?' asked the Queen.

'All the ordinary people,' said Polly, 'who'd never done you any harm. And the women, and the children, and the animals.'

'Don't you understand?' said the Queen (still speaking to Digory). 'I was the Queen. They were all *my* people. What else were they there for but to do my will?'

'It was rather hard luck on them, all the same,' said he.

'I had forgotten that you are only a common boy. How should you understand reasons of State? You must learn, child, that what would be wrong for you or for any of the common people is not wrong for a great Queen such as I. The weight of the world is on our shoulders. We must be freed from all rules. Ours is a high and lonely destiny.'

C. S. LEWIS, *The Magician's Nephew*

Bilbo Baggins

In a hole in the ground there lived a hobbit. Not a nasty, dirty, wet hole, filled with the ends of worms and an oozy smell, nor yet a dry, bare, sandy hole with nothing in it to sit down on or to eat: it was a hobbit-hole, and that means comfort.

It had a perfectly round door like a porthole, painted green, with a shiny yellow brass knob in the exact middle. The door opened on to a tube-shaped hall like a tunnel: a very comfortable tunnel without smoke, with panelled walls, and floors tiled and carpeted, provided with polished chairs, and lots and lots of pegs for hats and coats – the hobbit was fond of visitors. The tunnel wound on and on, going fairly but not quite straight into the side of the hill – and many little round doors opened out of it, first on one side and then on another. No going upstairs for the hobbit: bedrooms, bathrooms, cellars, pantries (lots of these), kitchens, dining-rooms, all were on the same floor, and indeed on the same passage. The best rooms were all on the left-hand side (going in), for these were the only ones to have windows, deep-set round windows looking over his garden, and meadows beyond, sloping down to the river.

This hobbit was a very well-to-do hobbit, and his name was Baggins. The Bagginses have lived in the neighbourhood of The Hill for time out of mind, and people considered them very respectable, not only because most of them were rich, but also because they never had any adventures or did anything unexpected: you could tell what a Baggins would say on any question without the bother of asking him. This is a story of how a Baggins had an adventure, and found himself doing and saying things altogether unexpected. He may have lost the neighbours' respect, but he gained – well, you will see whether he gained anything in the end.

The mother of our particular hobbit – what is a hobbit? I suppose hobbits need some description nowadays, since they have become rare and shy of the Big People, as they call us. They are (or were) a little people, about half our height, and smaller than the bearded dwarves. Hobbits have no beards. There is little or no magic about them, except the ordinary everyday sort which helps them to disappear quietly and quickly when large stupid folk like you and me come blundering along, making a noise like elephants which they can hear a mile off. They are inclined to be fat in the stomach; they dress in bright colours (chiefly green and yellow); wear no shoes, because their feet grow natural leathery soles and thick warm brown hair like the stuff on their heads (which is curly); have long clever brown fingers, good-natured faces, and laugh deep fruity laughs (especially after dinner, which they have twice a day when they can get it). Now you know enough to go on with. As I was saying, the mother of this hobbit – Bilbo Baggins, that is – was the famous Belladonna Took, one of the three remarkable daughters of the Old Took, head of the hobbits who lived across The Water, the small river that ran at the foot of The Hill. It was often said (in other families) that long ago one of the Took ancestors must have taken a fairy wife. That

was, of course, absurd, but certainly there was still something
not entirely hobbit-like about them, and once in a while
members of the Took-clan would go and have adventures.
They discreetly disappeared, and the family hushed it up; but
the fact remained that the Tooks were not as respectable as the
Bagginses, though they were undoubtedly richer.

Not that Belladonna Took ever had any adventures after
she became Mrs Bungo Baggins. Bungo, that was Bilbo's
father, built the most luxurious hobbit-hole for her (and partly
with her money) that was to be found either under The Hill
or over The Hill or across The Water, and there they remained
to the end of their days. Still it is probable that Bilbo, her only
son, although he looked and behaved exactly like a second
edition of his solid and comfortable father, got something a bit
queer in his makeup from the Took side, something that only
waited for a chance to come out. The chance never arrived,
until Bilbo Baggins was grown up, being about fifty years old
or so, and living in the beautiful hobbit-hole built by his
father, which I have just described for you, until he had in fact
apparently settled down immovably.

By some curious chance one morning long ago in the quiet
of the world, when there was less noise and more green, and the
hobbits were still numerous and prosperous, and Bilbo
Baggins was standing at his door after breakfast smoking an
enormous long wooden pipe that reached nearly down to his
woolly toes (neatly brushed) – Gandalf came by. Gandalf!
If you had heard only a quarter of what I have heard about
him, and I have only heard very little of all there is to hear,
you would be prepared for any sort of remarkable tale. Tales
and adventures sprouted up all over the place wherever he
went, in the most extraordinary fashion. He had not been
down that way under The Hill for ages and ages, not since his
friend the Old Took died, in fact, and the hobbits had almost
forgotten what he looked like. He had been away over The
Hill and across The Water on businesses of his own since
they were all small hobbit-boys and hobbit-girls.

All that the unsuspecting Bilbo saw that morning was an
old man with a staff. He had a tall pointed blue hat, a long
grey cloak, a silver scarf over which his long white beard
hung down below his waist, and immense black boots.

'Good Morning!' said Bilbo, and he meant it. The sun was
shining, and the grass was very green. But Gandalf looked at

him from under long bushy eyebrows that stuck out further
than the brim of his shady hat.

'What do you mean?' he said. 'Do you wish me a good
morning, or mean that it is a good morning whether I want it
or not; or that you feel good this morning; or that it is a
morning to be good on?'

'All of them at once,' said Bilbo. 'And a very fine morning
for a pipe of tobacco out of doors, into the bargain. If you have
a pipe about you, sit down and have a fill of mine! There's no
hurry, we have all the day before us!' Then Bilbo sat down on
a seat by his door, crossed his legs, and blew out a beautiful
grey ring of smoke that sailed up into the air without breaking
and floated away over The Hill.

'Very pretty!' said Gandalf. 'But I have no time to blow
smoke-rings this morning. I am looking for someone to share
in an adventure that I am arranging, and it's very difficult to
find anyone.'

'I should think so – in these parts! We are plain quiet folk
and have no use for adventures. Nasty disturbing uncomfortable things! Make you late for dinner! I can't think what anybody sees in them,' said our Mr Baggins, and stuck one thumb
behind his braces, and blew out another even bigger smoke-
ring. Then he took out his morning letters, and began to read,
pretending to take no more notice of the old man. He had
decided that he was not quite his sort, and wanted him to go
away. But the old man did not move. He stood leaning on his
stick and gazing at the hobbit without saying anything, till
Bilbo got quite uncomfortable and even a little cross.

'Good morning!' he said at last. 'We don't want any adventures here, thank you! You might try over The Hill or across
The Water.' By this he meant that the conversation was at an
end.

'What a lot of things you do use *Good morning* for!' said
Gandalf. 'Now you mean that you want to get rid of me, and
that it won't be good till I move off.'

'Not at all, not at all, my dear sir! Let me see, I don't think
I know your name?'

'Yes, yes, my dear sir – and I do know your name, Mr Bilbo
Baggins. And you do know my name, though you don't
remember that I belong to it. I am Gandalf, and Gandalf
means me! To think that I should have lived to be good-
morninged by Belladonna Took's son, as if I was selling

buttons at the door!'

'Gandalf, Gandalf! Good gracious me! Not the wandering wizard that gave Old Took a pair of magic diamond studs that fastened themselves and never came undone till ordered? Not the fellow who used to tell such wonderful tales at parties, about dragons and goblins and giants and the rescue of princesses and the unexpected luck of widows' sons? Not the man that used to make such particularly excellent fireworks! I remember those! Old Took used to have them on Midsummer's Eve. Splendid! They used to go up like great lilies and snapdragons and laburnums of fire and hang in the twilight all evening!' You will notice already that Mr Baggins was not quite so prosy as he liked to believe, also that he was very fond of flowers. 'Dear me!' he went on. 'Not the Gandalf who was responsible for so many quiet lads and lasses going off into the Blue for mad adventures? Anything from climbing trees to visiting elves – or sailing in ships, sailing to other shores! Bless me, life used to be quite inter – I mean, you used to upset things badly in these parts once upon a time. I beg your pardon, but I had no idea you were still in business.'

'Where else should I be?' said the wizard. 'All the same I am pleased to find you remember something about me. You seem to remember my fireworks kindly, at any rate, and that is not without hope. Indeed for your old grandfather Took's sake, and for the sake of poor Belladonna, I will give you what you asked for.'

'I beg your pardon, I haven't asked for anything!'

'Yes, you have! Twice now. My pardon. I give it you. In fact I will go so far as to send you on this adventure. Very amusing for me, very good for you – and profitable too, very likely, if you ever get over it.'

'Sorry! I don't want any adventures, thank you. Not today. Good morning! But please come to tea – any time you like! Why not tomorrow? Come tomorrow! Goodbye!' With that the hobbit turned and scuttled inside his round green door, and shut it as quickly as he dared, not to seem rude. Wizards after all are wizards.

'What on earth did I ask him to tea for!' he said to himself, as he went to the pantry. He had only just had breakfast, but he thought a cake or two and a drink of something would do him good after his fright.

Gandalf in the meantime was still standing outside the

door, and laughing long but quietly. After a while he stepped
up, and with the spike on his staff scratched a queer sign on the
hobbit's beautiful green front-door. Then he strode away,
just about the time when Bilbo was finishing his second cake
and beginning to think that he had escaped adventures very
well.

J. R. R. TOLKIEN, *The Hobbit*

The Elves of Sinadon

It was bleak on Mottram road under the Edge, the wooded
hill of Alderley. Trees roared high in the darkness. If any
people had cause to be out in the night, they kept their heads
deep in their collars, and their faces screwed blindly against
the Pennine wind. And it was as well they did, for among the
trees something was happening that was not meant for human
eyes.

From a rib of the Edge a shaft of blue light cut the darkness.
It came from a narrow opening in a high, tooth-shaped rock,
and within the opening was a pair of iron gates thrown wide,
and beyond them a tunnel. Shadows moved on the trees as a
strange procession entered through the gates and down into
the hill.

They were a small people, not more than four feet high,
deep-chested, with narrow waists, and long, slender arms and
legs. They wore short tunics, belted and sleeveless, and their
feet were bare. Some had cloaks of white eagle feathers, though
these were marks of rank rather than a protection. They
carried deeply curved bows, and from their belts hung on one
side quivers of white arrows, and on the other broad stabbing
swords. Each rode a small white horse, and some sat proudly
erect, though most drooped over the pommels of their
saddles, and a few lay irrevocably still across their horses'
necks, and the reins were held by others. All together they
numbered close on five hundred.

Beside the iron gates stood an old man. He was very tall,
and thin as a young birch tree. His white robes, and long white
hair and beard flew with the gale, and he held a white staff in
his hand.

Slowly the horsemen filed through the gates into the glim-
mering tunnel, and when they were all inside, the old man
turned, and followed them. The iron gates swung shut be-

hind him, and there was just a bare rock in the wind.

In this way the elves of Sinadon came unnoticed to Fundin-delve, last stronghold of the High Magic in our days, and were met by Cadellin Silverbrow, a great wizard, and guardian of the secret places of the Edge.

ALAN GARNER, *The Moon of Gomrath*

MAINLY SCIENTIFIC

A Blackbird is Hatched

In a cup-shaped nest of woven grass strengthened with mud and lined with more grass, the hen lays four or five eggs, bluish-green, freckled with reddish brown. As soon as the last egg is laid she begins to incubate. That is, except for short spells off the nest to ease her muscles, she sits tight on the eggs, the warmth from her body helping the growth within the shell. The cock brings her food and will sometimes take his turn at incubation, but the hen does most of it.

Each egg, like the hen's egg, with which we are more familiar, contains a rich yellow ball of yolk, surrounded by what we call the white of the egg. It is, in fact, not white until it is cooked. In the raw it is nearly transparent and acts as a protective cushion to the growing chick and the yolk on which it is nourished. When we crack a new-laid egg, all we see is yolk and white. The chick, or rather the beginnings of it, is there, but a microscope is needed to see the minute pin-point of life on the upper surface of the yolk. In a fortnight from the day the hen blackbird starts to incubate this pin-point grows in size over the surface of the yolk, until in the end of that time all that is left of the yolk is in the chick's stomach. While feeding on it, the chick has grown round it to enclose it.

The yolk is therefore a store of food provided in advance, which anticipates the young bird's needs. It is not the only way in which needs are provided in advance. Thus, the white of the eggs seems at first glance to be the same all through. In fact, there are two twisted ropes of the same transparent, jelly-like material, lying within it. One of these ropes is to one side of the spherical yolk and runs towards the narrow end of the shell. The other is on the opposite side of the yolk and runs towards the blunt end of the egg. We can see how these work if we take a disc of cardboard, make two holes near its centre, thread a string through the holes, and tie its ends to make a complete loop. With the finger of one hand through one loop of string, and a finger of the other hand through the other loop, we can spin the cardboard disc so that the string on either side of it becomes twisted. The tendency of twisted string is to untwist, and as it does so the cardboard on it spins. The force of the spin untwists the string but carries it on to twist in the opposite direction. So the disc is kept spinning first one way, then the other. The ropes in the white of the egg do something like this with the yolk, but much more gently. The effect is to keep the minute point of life, which is the growing chick, always uppermost, if the egg is rolled.

During incubation, the hen will, every now and then, rise on her feet within the nest, bend her head under her breast and, with her beak, turn each egg. Then she sits down on them again. She turns them so that no part of the egg shall be kept too warm or grow too cold. In the turning, the ropes in the white keep the growing chick uppermost, always at the point of maximum warmth. So the egg not only contains the growing chick and the food to feed it, but also a simple mechanism to keep the whole egg warm and to keep the chick itself warmest of all. It also has a hard shell to further protect the delicate chick, and this is, moreover, porous to allow air to pass through, for even at this very early stage a chick must have oxygen. One other thing may be mentioned. At the blunt end of the egg is a cavity, just inside the shell, filled with air. This contains the first gulp of air with which the young chick fills its lungs, just before it hatches.

A fortnight is a very short time for a minute speck of living protoplasm to grow into a nestling blackbird, so growth must be very rapid. There must be no mistakes. Everything must be prepared in advance and, if the growth and hatching are to succeed, everything to go according to plan. At the right time the chick must break out of the shell. To enable it to do this, there is a small horny tooth on the end of the beak, known as the egg tooth, which is shed soon after it has done its work.

At the end of the fortnight, the chick has the instinct – or, perhaps we had better say, feels an urge – to lift its head, break through into the cavity at the blunt end and gulp the air contained in it. It has now begun to use its lungs. Next it must crack the shell. This it does by punching a circle of holes with the egg tooth and pushing the cap of shell away. If you happen to be near at the right moment you can hear it chipping away at the shell. Finally it struggles out of the shell and lies helpless in the bottom of the nest. A young blackbird has been hatched.

MAURICE BURTON, *Animal Families*

Breeding Hamsters

Hamsters are old enough to breed at eight weeks and the female will continue to bear young for a year or so. By then hamsters are past their prime and, though they may live for two years or more, it is not good practice to breed old animals.

Once the male hamster is mature, it is ready to mate at any time. The female hamster is ready to mate every four days. Hamsters usually mate in the evenings. Place the female in the cage of the male towards evening. Mating should follow soon, and the female should be removed after an hour or so. If the pair fight and continue fighting, remove the female until another time.

Make a record of the date when mating takes place. The young will be born sixteen days later, perhaps less by three or four hours. Mark the date on a calendar and check. If your female is very tame, try to keep a record of her weight from the time she is mated till just before her young are born. Her weight may nearly double as the five to thirteen young develop inside her body. An average litter is six to eight.

Between the time of mating and the time the young are born, the female does not require special care. Give her a small dish of milk as well as her regular food. Keep this up after the young are born till they are able to care for themselves. The female will build her nest or will rebuild one she already has. Give her scraps of cloth or tissue paper to line her nest and make it softer and warmer. Do not handle or disturb the mother after the young are born, especially if it is her first litter. A frightened mother may kill her young and, for some reason, may eat them. Leave the mother alone for the first three or four days, if she has enough food and milk.

Even very tame hamsters are wilder just before and just after the young are born and are more likely to bite then. To clean the cage, coax the mother out by placing food in a tin

can. Set it on its side on the bottom of the cage. As the mother
enters to see what is there, lift the can with her inside. Some
mothers remain tame and do not mind being handled.

The blind, naked baby hamsters are very tiny. A litter of
eight to twelve weighs less than one ounce. But they grow
rapidly. In three days the skin begins to darken and hair
begins to appear. Eight-day-old babies begin to nibble at solid
food. At two weeks their eyes open and by that time they can
be handled as pets. Soon the mother stops nursing the young,
and when they are three or four weeks old, each baby hamster
weighs about an ounce and is on its own. The young should
then be separated from the mother, who is ready to have another family a month after the last litter was born. At five or
six weeks, young hamsters are old enough to breed, so males
and females should be separated before then.

HERBERT S. ZIM, *Golden Hamsters*

ACKNOWLEDGEMENTS

The authors and publishers wish to thank the following for permission to quote
copyright material: Tony Connor and Oxford University Press for 'Child's Bounc-
ing Song' from *Poems by Austin Clarke, Tony Connor and Charles Tomlinson*; Gerald
Duckworth Ltd for 'Godolphin Horne' from *Cautionary Tales* by Hilaire Belloc;
J. M. Dent & Sons Ltd for 'Adventures of Isabel' from *Family Reunion* by Ogden
Nash, for 'The Carpenter' from *Collected Poems* by Clifford Dyment and for extract
from *Sabotage at the Forge* by Richard Armstrong; Geoffrey Bles Ltd for 'Narnian
Suite' from *Poems* by C. S. Lewis; Faber & Faber Ltd for 'My Brother Bert', 'My
Grandpa' and 'My Sister Jane' from *Meet My Folks* by Ted Hughes, for 'The
Forge', 'Churning Day' from *Door into the Dark* by Seamus Heaney, for 'Old
Florist', 'The Meadow Mouse' and 'Orchids' from *Collected Poems* by Theodore
Roethke, for 'My Parents kept me from Children who were rough' from *Collected
Poems* by Stephen Spender; Rupert Hart-Davies Ltd and Gerald Durrell for
extracts from *My Family and Other Animals*; B. T. Batsford Ltd and Geraldine
Symons for extract from *Children in the Close*; Macmillan & Co. Ltd and the
Trustees of the Hardy Estate for 'Bags of Meat' from *Human Shows*; A. B. P.
International Ltd for 'Bats' by Randall Jarrell from *The Lost World* and for extracts
from *The American West* by J. A. Hawgood; Faber & Faber Ltd for extract from
A Stranger at Green Knowe by L. M. Boston; *The Guardian* for article by Judith
Cook; The Estate of the Late Mrs Frieda Lawrence and Laurence Pollinger Ltd
for extract from 'Fish' from *Collected Poems*, for extracts from *Sea and Sardinia*
and *Sons and Lovers*; Constable and Co. Ltd for 'The Cock Fight', 'New Corn',
'Green Green' and 'Sailing Homeward' from *170 Chinese Poems* translated by

Arthur Waley and for extracts from *The Log of a Cowboy* by Andy Adams; extract from *The People, Yes* by Carl Sandburg, copyright, 1936 by Harcourt Brace Jovanovich, Inc; renewed, 1964 by Carl Sandburg; 'Buffalo Dusk' from *Smoke and Steel* by Carl Sandburg, copyright, 1920, by Harcourt Brace Jovanovich, Inc; renewed, 1948, by Carl Sandburg; 'Winter Gold' from *Good Morning America*, copyright 1928, 1956 by Carl Sandburg; Holt Rinehart and Winston for 'Prairie' by Carl Sandburg from *Chicago Poems*; André Deutsch Ltd for extracts from *Shane* by Jack Schaefer; Macmillan & Co. Ltd for 'The Shell' by James Stephens and for 'The Ballad of the Frog Princess' by Charles Causley; Mischa Kudian for extract from translation of *Scenes from an Armenian Childhood* by Vahan Totovents; The Executors of the James Joyce Estate and The Bodley Head for extracts from *Ulysses*; Jonathan Cape Ltd for extract from *There Was a Time* by Walter Greenwood; Leslie Paul and Pergamon Press for extract from *The Boy down Kitchener Street*; The Literary Trustees of Walter de la Mare and The Society of Authors as their representative for 'The Listeners' from *The Complete Poems*; Macmillan and Co. Ltd for 'Flannan Isle' by W. W. Gibson; Hamish Hamilton Ltd for extract from *The 13 Clocks*, copyright © The Estate of James Thurber 1951; Penguin Books Ltd for extract from *Tales of the Greek Heroes* by Roger Lancelyn Green; Oxford University Press for 'The Lesson' from *A Tropical Childhood and other poems* by Edward Lucie-Smith; Faber & Faber Ltd for extract from *Little Children* by William Saroyan; Oxford University Press for 'Here' from *Rights of Passage* by Edward Braithwaite; Mrs Nicolette Gray and The Society of Authors, on behalf of the Laurence Binyon Estate for 'Hunger'; Hodder and Stoughton Ltd for extract from *A River Ran Out of Eden* by James Vance Marshall; Bantam Books Inc for 'The Sorrel Colt' by Benito Lynch, translated by Angel Flores, from *Spanish Stories*. A Bantam Dual-Language Book, edited by Angel Flores. © Copyright 1960 by Bantam Books Inc; MacGibbon and Kee Ltd for 'Children's Games' by William Carlos Williams from *Pictures from Brueghel*; The Executors of the James Joyce Estate and Jonathan Cape Ltd for extract from *A Portrait of the Artist as a Young Man*; MacGibbon & Kee Ltd for 'Here's a little mouse' by e. e. cummings; Rupert Hart-Davis Ltd for 'Lament for Prytherch' from *Song at the Year's Turning* by R. S. Thomas; Oxford University Press Ltd for extract from *A Grass Rope* by William Mayne; Harper & Row for extracts from *The Mass Media* by William Rivers; Michael Baldwin and Secker and Warburg Ltd for 'The Thing' from *Underneath*; Michael Joseph Ltd for extract from *Walkabout* by James Vance Marshall; The Bodley Head for extract from *The Magician's Nephew* by C. S. Lewis; George Allen and Unwin Ltd for extract from *The Hobbit* by J. R. R. Tolkien; William Collins & Sons Ltd for extract from *The Moon of Gomrath* by Alan Garner; Routledge & Kegan Paul Ltd for extract from *Animal Families* by Maurice Burton; World's Work for extract from *Golden Hamsters* by Herbert Zim; Laurence Pollinger Ltd for extract from 'Mother Goose' by Kenneth Rexroth from *The Collected Shorter Poems of Kenneth Rexroth*; The Centaur Press for 'Sir Roger is Dead' from 'An Old Woman Remembering' in *A Tale for the Fall of the Year and other Poems* by Margaret Stanley-Wrench; Curtis Brown Ltd and the Estate of Joyce Cary for extract from *To be a Pilgrim*; William Collins & Sons and Gerald Durrell for extract from *Birds, Beasts and Relatives*; Alan Brownjohn, The Digby Press and Macmillan & Co. Ltd for 'To See the Rabbit' by Alan Brownjohn from *The Railings*; Eyre & Spottiswoode Ltd and Spike Mays for extract from *Reuben's Corner*; Doubleday & Co. Inc. for extract from 'The Fun they Had' by Isaac Asimov; Chicago Daily News for 'Undersea Operation' by George Weller from issue of 14.12.42; Edward Arnold and Harry Graham for 'Auntie did you feel no pain' from *Ruthless Rhymes* by Harry Graham; Angus and Robertson for 'The Rainbow Bird' from *Rainbow Bird and Other Stories* by Vance Palmer; Penguin Books Ltd for extract from *The Swindler* by Francisco de Quevedo trans. Michael Alpert from *Two Spanish Picaresque Novels*.